Creative Activities
for Developing
Emotional
Intelligence

Creative Activities for Developing Emotional Intelligence

HINTON HOUSE Emotional Literacy Resources

Sue Jennings

HINTONHOUSE

Illustrations for worksheets by George Johnson and Tangle Design (worksheets 3–8).

First published in 2013 by

Hinton House Publishers Ltd,

Newman House, 4 High Street, Buckingham, MK18 1NT, UK

T +44 (0)1280 822557   F +44 (0)560 313 5274
E info@hintonpublishers.com

www.hintonpublishers.com

British Library Cataloguing in Publication Data

Jennings, Sue.
    101 activities for empathy & awareness. – (101 activities & ideas)
    1. Emotional problems of children. 2. Emotional problems of teenagers. 3. Emotional intelligence–Study and teaching. 4. Social perception--Study and teaching. 5. Respect for persons–Study and teaching. 6. Self-consciousness (Awareness)–Study and teaching.
    I. Title II. Series III. One hundred and one activities for empathy & awareness IV. Hundred and one activities for empathy & awareness
    155.4'124-dc22

ISBN 978 1 906531 48 5

Printed and bound in the United Kingdom by Hobbs the Printers Ltd

Contents

Contents

Contents

Resources

Resources

Acknowledgements

My thanks to George Johnson for working under pressure for the illustrations, and to my clients for allowing me to use examples of their situations.

The Rowan Tree Trust has given me time and space for working this book.

As ever, I would like to thank Sarah Miles for being a very patient publisher!

Sue Jennings
UK & Malaysia
2013

About the Author

Sue Jennings PhD is a play and dramatherapist, storyteller and performer. She is the author of many books, a number of which are published by Hinton House. In 2012 Sue was awarded a Churchill Fellowship for research into 'Arts and Elderly People' which enabled her travel to Malaysia, Romania and Czech Republic.

She is Visiting Fellow at Leeds Metropolitan University and Project Director for UK charity Rowan Tree Trust. Sue is passionate about play, drama and children's attachment and development. Her 'Embodiment-Projection-Role' (EPR) paradigm, as described in this book, is used in education and therapy as a means of structuring play and story activities, as well as research and measurement.

Sue works regularly with children in orphanages in Romania and trains care staff from institutions. Her current work is developing 'Neuro-Dramatic-Play' in therapeutic play for children with attachment difficulties.

Introduction

This book is written for parents (including foster carers) and teachers, as well as all of the different people who give children and young people care at different stages in their lives. This includes counsellors and therapists, care workers, teaching assistants, family support workers, 'buddies' and 'befrienders'. All of these people are required to care for children and young people and also to support them into some sort of pleasure in living. Their lives may not be ideal, but to be able to develop the capacity to have their basic needs met, their emotional lives understood, and the possibility of some hope and optimism for the future, is surely in the interests of everyone. Through working to improve the Emotional Intelligence of children and young people, we are supporting them to have some control over their emotions and not to be overwhelmed by them, as well as to be able to express them in appropriate contexts and to understand the emotions of others. This leads us to consider the big questions of empathy and awareness (Jennings, 2011c).

What is Emotional Intelligence?

So what do we mean by the term Emotional Intelligence (EI)? Different writers discuss 'Emotional Quotient' (EQ) (Stein, 2009), 'Emotional Literacy' (Steiner, 2003), 'Social Intelligence' (Goleman, 2006) and 'Emotional IQ' (Goleman, 2004; Bradberry, Greaves & Lencioni, 2009). For the purpose of this book I am referring to the capacity of children, teenagers and adults to 'manage their emotions appropriately'. This means a degree of awareness of the responses that are appropriate in any given situation. For example, as we grow up we learn to express sympathy towards someone if their partner has died, to communicate pleasure for a celebration of a person's graduation, or to react with wonder when something that seems magical appears. As babies and children develop they learn about these feelings from the people around them and from stories that are told about events that have happened.

The joy at the arrival of a new baby usually overrides the pain that may be experienced during the birth. However, the feeling of hopelessness if a baby was not wished for, or the despair for an already overcrowded, impoverished family, or the guilt and anxiety if the child was conceived from an extra-marital liaison may be communicated to the infant and affect their emotional development. Similarly, children who are conceived and born into families where there is domestic violence, extreme neglect or substance abuse may be confused about the expression of feelings and their consequences. For example, the following description illustrates what I term the 'tiptoe child'.

Case study 1

Jamie is the elder of two children and was born into a family of alcohol excess. He was the reason for the marriage, since his mother had escaped from a tyrannical father only to feel she was now trapped in the tyranny of an 'enforced' marriage. Jamie sought help as a young adult because he was struggling with attempts to form relationships that always started very optimistically and then broke down in confusion and chaos, and the feeling reported afterwards was one of being lost. We worked with his early experiences using Worksheets 2 'Relationship Circles' and 14 'A Feelings Map', and he arrived at some very important insights. He extended this new understanding into some sand-play work (see Resources: Notes on Sand Play).

Jamie realised that all of his early memories were connected with his mother's alcohol abuse. He felt he was treading on eggshells when he came home from school, because he never knew how his mother might react: she could be abusive and accusing if she was without a drink, or completely effusive and 'sloppy and huggy' if she was drunk, or 'out of it' if she was extremely drunk. He realised that he was used to being the strong one, comforting his younger sister when she became distressed and seeing to his mother's demands or anticipating her demands if she had become incoherent. Consequently he now realised that he went into relationships 'as a carer', saying that this was the only role he knew; but really he wanted to be cared *for*, as he had never experienced that in his life. In his relationships with others he had swung between being caring and demanding, and he had never understood the causes until now. Through the EI work he was able to get in touch with the destructive anger he felt as a teenager at having to lead an 'abnormal life'; he had begun to go on drinking binges and had become promiscuous, which would be followed by periods of total austerity to punish himself for the times he was out of control. By using Worksheet 14 'A Feelings Map', he was able to see the limitations of his emotional expression, and the way in which his feelings were a direct response to his early neglect. He no longer needed to 'tiptoe' around other people, especially women, for fear of unpredictable reactions.

Case study 2

This case study illustrates the complex needs of children and young people who have an impoverished emotional intelligence. Janet was 10 years old and had a big beam of a smile, but always a worried frown. She had learning difficulties, lived at home and attended a special school. She always needed feedback that everything was all right, and constantly asked whether I needed any help. She would tug at my sleeve, asking what she could do, or was I all right, or should she clean up. Messy play activities initially made her very anxious and she would keep looking for reassurance that it was acceptable to put her fingers in the paint or the clay, and that she did not have to rush to get the wipes to clean her hands. She attended a programme of workshops for children who all had difficulties in dealing with their emotional needs and struggled to express them appropriately to match the circumstances. She was supported to explore messy play activities and slowly to take risks in the physical games such as the Drama & Focus Games in the Resources section. Staff encouraged her to say what she would like to do, rather than to follow what she thought we wanted her to do. She was failing to internalise both self-esteem and confidence, which is an essential process in the development of emotional intelligence.

It is important to remember that the basis of many difficulties in the development of emotional intelligence is that emotional responses and experiences have never been established in early infancy, or have been muddled and confused. In order to grasp the roots of this work, it is essential that we revisit attachment theory.

Understanding Attachment

Contemporary thinking has been permanently influenced by the original attachment theorist, John Bowlby. His seminal works (1965, 2005 [1979]) have enabled us to understand that the early relationship between an infant and principal carer has a lasting influence on the development of both the brain and the emotional life of children and therefore young people. Indeed we could say that the brain houses the emotions, and neuroscientists have shown that certain areas of the brain will not develop unless there is a satisfactory level of emotional interaction between infant and carer (Cozolino, 2002; Jennings 2011a). Attachment is what used to be called 'bonding' between parent and child, but it is only in recent years that its importance has been demonstrated scientifically (Sunderland, 2006).

It is through the early healthy attachment relationship that infants will develop trust, hope (Erikson, 1995 [1950]), affirmation and confidence. Erikson focuses on the quality of interactions between parents and children, and says that if the small infant experiences 'warmth, regularity and dependable affection' then their view of the world will be one of trust and thus hope. He is describing the basic qualities of attachment between mother and child.

Frequent contact with the body of the adult carer will allow the infant to develop a sense of their own body outline and balance, while sensory play will heighten sensory responses that feed straight into the emotions. The sequencing of 'sensory, rhythmic and dramatic play' (Jennings, 2011a) allows the infant to become playful, responsive and interactive. For the infant who has not had these experiences, it is necessary to look at the potential emotional deficits. For many of the damaged children the first 'trust versus mistrust' stage in Erickson's theory has not taken place. A host of other fearful experiences have entered the amygdala (the area of the brain associated with processing memory and emotional reactions), creating a self-perpetuating situation of Reactive Attachment Condition (Hughes, 2006). Gerhardt, (2004) uses the phrase 'emotional immunity' to describe the positive affective development of babies and infants: 'Good emotional "immunity" comes out of the experience of feeling safely held, touched, seen and helped to recover from stress, whilst the stress response is undermined by separation, uncertainty, lack of contact and lack of regulation.'

The development of our brains and the maturation of our emotions are therefore dependent on our early playful attachment. This loving interaction is a two-way communication, at first through touch, sound, rhythm and gaze. The emotional interaction influences the growth of the brain and without it the brain will not fully develop.

The Playful Brain

The brain has enormous potential for learning and storing and for shaping most areas of development, a potential unknown until recent years when the work of neuroscientists became more widespread (Damasio, 2000).

It is useful to consider that the instinctual, or reptilian, area of the brain that includes the amygdala is where fears, both inherited and acquired, are stored. The emotional or mammalian brain is concerned with nurture and feeding. This is shared by all mammals, and probably contributes to attachment and the care of small infants.

The rational brain, also referred to as the higher brain, which is the seat of executive function, is where our lived and conscious experience is located, together with our informed decision-making and reflection.

The instinctual brain reacts to danger and those children who have had early fearful experiences can have many intense reactions that are stored in their amygdalae. For example, the child who has been threatened with violence from an adult in close proximity may well react with fear at the closeness of any adult.

The emotional brain is located in the limbic system and, as its name suggests, is involved with the emotions as well as learning and memory. The higher brain is within the neocortex. Because this area of the brain is still 'soft-wired' at birth (in other words not all the synaptic connections have been formed), it will be affected by external influences in parenting and care. Loving interactions, affirmation and playfulness will have a strong influence on the growth of the higher brain and its functions. It is responsible not only for empathy, but also for imagination, problem-solving and the capacity to reflect. However, the rational brain needs to work in collaboration with other parts of the brain and not separately from the 'emotional brain' or the 'instinctual brain'. The child who is sent to their room when they are thought to be 'out of control' will only develop further feelings of fear and isolation, and is likely to have toxic chemicals flooding their brain (Sunderland, 2006). The child who is held firmly and warmly when thought to be 'beyond themselves', will feel more secure and 'held' while they recover their equilibrium.

Whereas sensory play (for example, through touch and massage, soothing sounds and loving gestures and words) strengthens the emotional areas of the brain including the thalamus and the hypothalamus, dramatic play helps to develop the potential for empathy that belongs to the higher brain areas.

It is also important to know about the mirror neurons in the brain. Mirror neurons fire when humans and other animals perform specific actions *and* when they see another perform the same action. Babies at 36 hours old can differentiate between happy, sad and surprised human facial expressions. Within the first few hours of birth, new-born babies can imitate their mother's expression and even stick out their tongues.

The mirror neurons are responsible for an infant learning social and emotional responses and form the basis of collaboration, setting a good example, and group rituals and dancing.

Empathy & Awareness

If a child has developed empathy in the early stages, through their principal carer being 'attuned' to the feelings of the child and responding accordingly, then as they develop they, too, will learn to understand the feelings of another person. A carer who responds to a baby's distress or to their joy is laying the foundation of the child's capacity to empathise. A child who is ignored or who is smacked for crying will grow up both emotionally confused and lacking in genuine empathy. A person cannot express empathy unless they have experienced it themselves (see Jennings, 2011c).

It is very helpful to make use of dramatic play and role play when working with emotions, because they both promote the capacity to step out of one's own personal reality and to enter that of someone else. It is only through being able to play dramatically, to take on roles in thought or action, that we are able to consider the feelings and experiences of somebody else. This is how we develop empathy and the child who cannot engage in dramatic playing will have great difficulty with understanding the 'other'.

Empathy is also linked to the development of a conscience. Our moral sense and our values are linked to how we treat other people. Empathy is the ability to stand in someone else's shoes and to understand how they feel. We cannot empathise unless we can 'take on the role of the other' (Mead, 1934).

Embodiment-Projection-Role: a Working Model for Emotional Intelligence

The Embodiment-Projection-Role (EPR) model of emotional intelligence charts the 'dramatic development' of children from birth to seven years of age (Jennings, 1990; 1998; 1999). The three stages of EPR and their appropriate transitions are essential for the healthy development and maturation of children. They influence the development of both the right and left hemispheres of the brain, as well as supporting emotional intelligence and self-confidence. If children do not navigate the stages of EPR successfully, this can have serious consequences in later life. For example, a child who has not been able to go through an appropriate embodied stage (E) may have a distorted body image and the potential to develop eating disorders. A child who struggles with hand-eye coordination and literacy, and perhaps has little confidence in their own artistic abilities, may well have never been through the projective stage (P). There are many children who are unable to 'pretend' (in other words, to take on the role of another, be it animal or person), because they have not been through the role stage (R) of development. They may then play out destructive or isolated roles in everyday life. Such children have not only missed out the role stage of EPR, but also the time of dramatic playing during the early weeks and months. They are unable to dramatise their roles, but continue their lives in a series of destructive day-to-day encounters where they often play the role of aggressor or victim.

I have worked with children who will happily play at physical games or movement exercises (Sherborne, 2001), or who will create collage or self-portraits or intricate clay models, but they have been quite unable to play a role, that is, to become someone other than themselves (Jennings, 2008). To play a role means that we are able to play 'as if' we are the other person (or creature). This is what I term 'the dramatic response' (Jennings, 2011a), and to respond 'as if' we are someone else, both as child or young person, informs how we respond, plan and negotiate our lives (Hickson, 2011).

How EPR Works in Practice

This book is designed to assist children and young people through the developmental stages that enable them to become emotionally (and later socially) intelligent. Embodied, projective and role exercises that are carefully graded make sure that the individual and group build, in laddered structures, a foundation for healthy emotional growth. For example, the 'tiptoe child' described above needs to build confidence in his or her body, to grow in stature and find a balance, before they develop the ability to communicate feelings. Sessions that involve 'stop-start' games, such as Grandmother's Footsteps, or physical interactions such as Push Me – Pull You (see Resources: Drama & Focus Games), pay attention to the embodied stage, before moving to the projective stage, which can be linked to the body. For example, drawing around the hand and showing what it can be used for increases confidence in drawing and also shows a variety of positive activities for hands. Once a child has persevered with embodied and projective exercises, simple role techniques can be introduced, such as dramatising the story of 'The Child who Disappeared' (Resources: Stories & Storytelling, Story Sheet 4).

The three stages of EPR and their appropriate transitions are essential for the healthy development and maturation of emotions. They influence the development of both the right and left hemispheres of the brain as well as encouraging resilience and self confidence. If children do not navigate the EPR stages it may have serious consequences in later life. Indeed a child who has not been able to go through an appropriate embodied stage (0 – 12 months) may have a distorted body image and potential eating disorders. A child who struggles with hand-eye coordination and literacy, and maybe has little confidence in their own artistic abilities, may never have traversed the projective stage (13 months – 3 years). Many children, teenagers (and adults) are unable to 'pretend' i.e. to take on the role of another (be it animal or person), because they have not been through the role stage, (3-6 years) and will then play out destructive or isolated roles in everyday life, and have difficulties in managing their feelings.

These children and teenagers have not only missed out the role stage of EPR, but also the time of dramatic playing during the early weeks and months after birth. They are unable to dramatise their roles but continue life in a series of day-to-day destructive encounters where they often play out roles of aggressors or victims. Some children will happily play at physical games or movement exercises (Sherborne 2001) or will create collage or self portraits or intricate clay models, but they have been quite unable to play a role i.e. to become someone other than themselves. To play a role means that we are able to play 'as if' we are the other person (or creature). It is a transition from everyday reality to dramatic reality (Jennings 1990, Pendzik 2008). This is what I term 'the dramatic response' (Jennings 1998), and it is only through being able to play dramatically, to take on roles in the imagination or action, that we are able to consider the feelings and experiences of somebody else. This is how we develop empathy and the child who cannot engage in dramatic playing will have great difficulty with understanding 'the other'.

Working on the premise that EPR is an accurate observation of the stages of dramatic development, it therefore follows coherently, that EPR as a therapy can enable a re-working of missed experiences in order for children or adults to make-good some, if not all, of their developmental deficit.

Therefore the following hypothesis for practice is that EPR can be applied as an assessment and recording procedure, in order to determine areas of deficit. For example, a child of 10 years who persistently sits in a corner and sucks a thumb, rocks and dribbles, could be displaying developmental delay in all areas: physical, emotional, intellectual, imaginative, dramatic and social. If we also observe that the child does not respond to soft toys, puzzles, play dough but was noticing the blowing of bubbles and the singing of a lullaby, there is already information to start our assessment. Looking at the EPR record & assessment sheets 1–4 (Worksheets 18–21), it is likely that sheets 3 and 4 (Worksheets 20 and 21) will not have responses for this child, and the detail will focus on sheets 1 'Day-to-Day Embodiment' (Worksheet 18), and 2 'Creative Embodiment' (Worksheet 19).

Although the child is displaying a range of physical, embodied actions, the EPR recording sheets do not have enough detail in order to record a comprehensive assessment. Although EPR has broad-based categories, they do not include enough information to include early sensory play for example (Jennings 2012c).

There are recording and assessment sheets (Worksheets 18–21) to write down observations of EPR activity. The charts can be used purely for observation which then allows practitioners to keep an eye on children's and teenager's progress. The worksheets can also be used for assessment before sessions commence to ascertain the emotional stage of a child or teenager. It is helpful to remember that the child or young person who will not or cannot play a role is likely to need more embodiment and more projection experience before undertaking role activities.

Sand Play: a joyous technique

Sand Play as a means of educational and therapeutic intervention is a very important technique because of its flexibility and adaptability for children and teenagers. Sand Play incorporates embodiment (because sand is sensory to the touch), projection (because it is 'out there', like a picture), and also role (because dramas, scenes and stories can be portrayed through small objects and figures). There is a description of basic Sand Play equipment in the Resources section.

The use of sand connects with an individual's most basic feelings and allows them to 'start all over'. It does seem that even the most difficult teenager will respond to Sand Play. They connect with the sand itself, are intrigued by the diversity of the small figures and intuitively discover a means of concretising what they need to express. Whereas with younger children there is usually a wish to create 'messy play' using sand and water, older children and teenagers are less likely to be tactile in this way, and find in the sand a means of constructing a picture or story. Indeed the picture itself can portray a total mess, or chaos or confusion.

I have not attempted individual sand trays with a whole class of children, but I find that group sand trays, five children to a tray for Storybuilding (Jennings, 2010), works for collaborative story development. There are increasing ideas for expanding Sand Play in education (Smith, 2012), but here I wish to focus specifically on its relationship with the growth of emotional intelligence. Many children and teenagers struggle to find the words, and adults become exasperated by monosyllables and grunts! The very essence of play and drama, which is to show rather then tell, bypasses this demand for language, especially concerning someone's feelings. A picture in the sand tray conveys both subtlety and nuance in the individual's expression, which may, in time, become a story.

Case study 3

Tom would not engage with anything about school, and would turn away from everyone and everything, with no eye contact. He was in a foster placement, having been removed from the family home when it was discovered that he had been locked in a garden shed at night because his mother said he 'was too much bother'. She encouraged his older siblings to bully him. He initially came for individual Sand Play work to see if he could find any means of expressing his feelings, and he spent time running his fingers through the sand, then pouring water and making it splash. Nearby was a large hourglass, which he looked at and turned over to watch the sand trickling through. He made a bending river shape in the sand, placed a bridge across the river, and then chose some bits of twig to create another bridge (this image was the inspiration for Worksheet 3 'Bridges'). He then said, quite simply, with fleeting eye contact, 'In this story there is a choice.' This was his first communication, verbal and non-verbal. Over time he was able to articulate his feelings in stories that made use of landscapes: empty and barren, water out of control, and cliffs that were steep; various human figures with their backs turned towards a small wild boar that was later replaced by a wolf.

By being kept out of human contact for long periods of time and then being treated with violence, Tom had never experienced or learned any emotions apart from fear. He had no language of feelings, but was able to slowly build this up both by telling and having told to him stories that included appropriate emotional reactions to different situations.

A Range of Emotional Struggles for Children and Young People

There is a range of emotional struggles that many children and young people experience, and ways in which to assist them will form the substance of the practical sections of this book.

1   The troubled child or young person (5 aspects):
    loner, rager, reactor, tiptoe, shut-down

2   The anxious child or young person (5 aspects):
    helper, predictor, vigilante, perfector, self-harmer

3   The energised child or young person (5 aspects):
    boxer, blocker, dropper, over-the-top, destroyer

There are also five aspects that are potentials for change, as a result of applied strategies for Emotional Intelligence.

4 The calm child or young person (5 aspects):
reflector, day-dreamer, perseverer, industrialist, artist

5 The sparkling child or young person (5 aspects):
explorer, high-fiver, interactor, joker, creator

For example, a child who is 'shut-down' (who will not respond to other people, adults or children and has difficulty communicating) should not be expected to become a 'high-fiver', with lots of energy, perhaps extrovert, and someone who will initiate ideas. Rather we would hope they will become less troubled and calmer, and will reduce their fears and discover some joy.

Equally, a teenager who blocks every attempt to reach him or her may slowly find a way of interacting with, and using, that energy. They are unlikely to sit still and reflect, certainly in the early stages of change.

It is important that we consider appropriate methods in order to address the needs of the child or young person, as well as being mindful of a realistic outcome.

A Mindful Approach
Much has been written about mindfulness (Gunaratana 2002, Siegal 2007, Williams 2007) and, although there are many books available now, mindfulness is a very ancient concept and its principles have permeated much religious practice and philosophy. It is not difficult to see why interest in mindfulness is increasing when we reflect on the greater and greater pressures on people to achieve, the large numbers of teenagers who are disaffected, and the undoubted increase in self-destructive and other harmful behaviours. More than fifty years ago Anthony Newley and Anna Quale starred in the musical *Stop the World – I Want to Get Off!* (1961); this phrase challenged my own thinking, even then.

A mindful approach towards Emotional Intelligence allows us to consider the possibility of looking at emotions in other ways. For example, it is often thought that children are immature in their emotional development, or they are unable to express their emotions, or that they allow their emotions to rule their lives. So either we devise ways for them to 'catch up', or insist that it is good for them to express their feelings, or give them medication 'to calm them down'. A mindful approach could take into consideration the larger emotional map of the child or teenager.

The children who are described in the case studies in this book could have various issues to address: perhaps a child has not been allowed to mature emotionally and has been kept a child. This can happen for many reasons, including a parent's fear of losing a child, anxiety that they will get into trouble once they are a teenager, or that staying 'my baby' gives emotional justification to the needs of a parent. The teenager who does not express their feelings may well have witnessed only violent emotions in the home or been a victim of uncontrolled or excess emotions from an adult. The child or teenager who is thought to have 'out-of-control' emotions may have never been 'contained' as a child, a process in which emotional boundaries are learned through appropriate attachment.

Being mindful is to develop a greater awareness of ourselves and others, especially when we are used to being on automatic pilot. For example, it is easy to assume that someone is engaged in 'mindless destruction' rather than understanding that possibly the person's mindfulness has become distorted. Exposure to frequent images of gratuitous violence must surely affect the mirror neurons of an individual's brain, so that violence is integrated into their brain as the norm thereby distorting the mindfulness. As educators we become seduced into 'hurry up and finish', or 'the first to finish puts up their hand', or 'we are working to the stop-watch' attitudes, as if the whole of life has become a race. Mindfulness is in the moment, not about the unhappy past or the scary future, but the here and now. Mindfulness is fed by the senses: what do I see, hear, smell, taste and feel, and it is a gradual process. Sometimes one can start a group by asking everyone to take a deep breath and then say the first thing that comes to mind. It will usually be linked to something they are sensing!

How to Use this Book

The Structure of the Book

This is a book of ideas and techniques, as well as suggestions for their application to a range of children and young people who face struggles expressing their emotions.

There are four main parts in the book:

Part 1: Faces & Feelings: Understanding & Recognising our Emotions, including the use of Sand Play.

Part 2: Embodiment Activities. Physical exercises, strategies and games for children and young people, including suggestions for variations.

Part 3: Projective Activities. Techniques involving painting and drawing, collage and magazine work, including suggestions for variations.

Part 4: Role Activities. Drama exercises, scenes and stories for simple enactment and sharing.

Part 5: Resources. These include:

- ✿ Worksheets to accompany the exercises, including record sheets, certificates and assessments.
- ✿ Stories and storytelling techniques for exploration and for reading within the sessions.
- ✿ Drama and focus games to integrate within the sessions or to use as preliminaries for drama work.
- ✿ Useful reading and websites.

It is suggested that the sections are worked through developmentally.

Part 1 is used to familiarise participants with the language of emotions, using activities based on the pictorial representation of faces and their feelings and Worksheets 3–8 'Recognising Primary Feelings'. Sand Play is also recommended, but not obligatory, as an introductory activity.

Parts 2, 3 and 4 follow the sequencing of Embodiment-Projection-Role, and it is usual that role work cannot develop unless the embodiment milestones have been achieved. A child who has not developed within their own body will struggle with playing the role of someone else. A teenager who has not experienced physical containment will find it difficult to contain themselves within a drawing or painting.

However, the activities are not rigid in their sequencing and if the embodiment boundaries are well established, activities from other sections can be tested out. Nevertheless, it is important to establish a rhythm of warm-up and closure that helps the group or individual to both manage their emotions and then to make the transition to other classes or groups.

Important points to note when working with feelings
Intensive work on feelings and emotions is very tiring and can make people feel vulnerable. Therefore the pace of the sessions needs gauging carefully. Space out the activities and worksheets and intersperse them with material from Drama & Focus Games and Stories & Storytelling in the Resources section. The use of these additional resources will also ensure that there is enough material to sustain a session and to cover any contingencies. Ensure that there is plenty of restorative time so that participants feel comfortable about moving on to further activities.

Disclosures
When working with emotions, there will be times when children and young people are in touch with feelings that may be too powerful to be addressed in the group. It is important to acknowledge the feelings, provide a supportive environment, and to suggest a meeting afterwards where you can recommend seeing the school counsellor or pastoral care worker. If abuse is disclosed then it is essential to follow the school's policy and report to the relevant authority.

Support for Teachers, Carers & Therapists

When we are addressing issues of emotions and feelings, often expressed in extreme ways, it is easy to forget the toll that this takes on the adults in question. Many of the extreme emotions are expressed directly to the group or individual facilitators and, however prepared we might be, it is exhausting nevertheless. We do have to keep telling ourselves 'not to take it personally', in spite of the fact that at one level we already know this.

Support from others

It is so important that we are able to acknowledge that we need support from our peers. Fellow teachers and carers are also experiencing similar struggles, and no one should have to paste on a brave face just because they are feeling metaphorically bruised or battered (and in some situations there could be actual physical or emotional violence).

Recently I was asked to run a course on 'Attachment and Loss for Carers in Care Homes', and the manager of the care home suggested it might be a good idea if she opened the session with a few words of her own. Turning to the group of a dozen carers (who were all working in the dementia care unit), she said, 'We have all had a very difficult week; colleagues have been overstretched because of absence for illness, and I know you are feeling the loss of three of our residents. I propose that we have a treat: I have ordered bacon sandwiches and fresh coffee for everyone.' And, yes, there were alternatives for vegetarians! But it was an act of spontaneous kindness, and her acknowledgement of the demands and difficulties made such a difference. And all the carers were really motivated to participate in the course.

Supervision for therapists

All therapists are required to have regular supervision, and a good supervisor will also be mindful when someone is getting stressed or overwhelmed. However, it is a human failing that we tend to feel we are 'not coping' if we admit to being tired or tearful, or generally not 'on the ball'. Increasingly teachers are realising that supervision, far from being an admission that they cannot do their job, is a means of enhancing their practice, as well as being very supportive.

What can we do for ourselves?

There are various exercises described in this book that we can use for our own support and growth. Many of the movement and drawing techniques we can use just to let off steam. A regular movement class of yoga, Pilates or jazz dance always seems to keep everything in perspective. Personally, I have a weekly singing lesson and it seems to 'even me out'.

Deep breathing exercises are also to be recommended, especially when children or teenagers put us under stress and we instinctively want to respond. If we react, the behaviour will usually escalate (see Jennings, 2013), so we need to develop strategies to self-sooth and stay calm. A very good idea is to have one's own sand-tray at home and a collection of small figures and objects. The sand itself is very calming when fingers are run through it, and the objects can be used to create pictures of how you are feeling, or even to solve difficulties. It is putting everything 'out there', and by using small objects to represent difficult decisions that we need to make, we can get a better perspective and even look at potential outcomes.

Soothing objects to contemplate (such as aquariums or mobiles) help to de-stress most people; TV unfortunately has the opposite effect, because the flickering images agitate the brain. However, we can always get out of doors for walks, or perhaps spend some time in the garden. Even two or three plants in pots that blossom throughout the seasons can serve the same purpose.

The other thing we can do for ourselves is to take time out: to do enjoyable things in our spare time and to keep up hobbies and interests. It is easy when we are stressed to let things slide and tell ourselves that we need time for marking, writing reports, filling in forms: in fact a whole multitude of tasks that undermine our well-being.

Let these thoughts be your motto:

No form is important enough to lose sleep over.
No report is important enough to sabotage our well-being.

Part 1
Faces & Feelings: Understanding & Recognising our Emotions

Sand Play

Activities for Recognising Primary Feelings

1   Newspaper Feelings

2   Name the Feelings

3   Draw the Feelings

4   Primary Feelings

Moving On

It is recommended that ideas arising from this section are explored before beginning work on the main sections (Embodiment, Projection and Role) of this book. This is to support both the language of feelings as well the visual cues that go with a feeling. For many children and young people their feelings become a mass of uncontrolled expression (Jennings, 2012b) that pours out onto anyone nearby. Many of these young people are unable to differentiate between degrees of intensity in their feelings, and will use a single word or phrase, such as 'bad' or 'dead-like' or 'crazy' or 'shit' or 'rough'. The more we try to insist that they define themselves, the more we get frustrated and the young people shut down.

However, it may be that useful work can be achieved through the use of Sand Play as a means of accessing feelings and stories before these activities are introduced. This is very much an individual decision and depends on the availability of suitable resources and knowledge of the participating group. It should be emphasised that this is not sand-tray therapy or play therapy through Sand Play. It is a means of using an individual's potential for playing with a primary substance as a way of accessing their emotions and creating of pictures and stories.

Sand Play

Preparation   It is important that time is spent to focus concentration and energy through the use of some breathing exercises (see Resources p. 113). Calming music can accompany this work, but experience has shown that very often the sand itself is a calming medium.

Young children: Utilise existing sand equipment and encourage sensory play with sand and water, mixing and modelling, pouring and splashing. Children usually like to bury their hands, build tunnels and create castles. Non-intrusive questions can encourage the expression of how the sand feels, when it is wet and dry, when hands are buried, and so on. Write down the 'feeling' words on a board in order that the children remember them.

Encourage the creation of landscapes with stones, shells, bark, leaves, fossils, pebbles, ensuring that as many textures as possible are available. Encourage the expression of words to describe the objects and then a short story about the landscape.

If the children are ready, use small figures of people, animals etc., and invite them to create a picture and then tell a story. Allow 10 to 15 minutes for the making of the picture and then 5 minutes for sharing the story. Careful questions can assist the emotional expressions ('And how did the tiger feel when the boy shouted at him?'). It is important to allow time for disengagement from the activity: the objects can be put away and the sand smoothed to finish.

Older children and young people are less likely to want the messy play (there are exceptions!) and individual sand trays are recommended with a selection of all the objects suggested above.

Newspaper Feelings

A very simple exercise can help to test a young person's ability to recognise degrees of emotion.

Bring in some newspaper headlines, cut from a range of publications, which make strong, emotive statements. For example:

✿ Businessman cheats bankers and blames wife!

✿ England celebrates yet another success.

✿ Missing child – still no news after five days.

✿ Strike action called after worker blamed for accident and subsequently found innocent.

✿ Teenager arrested for murder of shopkeeper.

✿ Vicar is trying to encourage young people to church social groups.

Ask the group to sit in a circle and then everyone can look at a headline and comment on it. Make sure everyone can read, or that the headlines are read out, before anyone is expected to speak. Encourage people to comment on how they feel and perhaps to elaborate on the story. No one should feel 'put on the spot', instead that they can contribute to something in the media with their own comments (and feelings). People may feel sorry, angry, worried, disgusted, and so on.

This type of exercise enables children and teenagers to recognise feelings about other people or an incident without being asked directly, 'What are you feeling?' (which usually results in 'Dunno'). At least 'feeling' words are now being acknowledged.

2 Name the Feelings

Using a large whiteboard and coloured markers, invite group members to call out 'feeling' words; do not ask for words that describe how they are currently feeling, but just use the words they suggest to create a list on the board.

When the list is complete, discuss with group members when and why people might have those sorts of feelings; make sure the discussion is kept in the third person and de-personalised. That way no one will feel under threat of having to say something about themselves, but feelings are being named and the language of feelings is being acknowledged.

Draw the Feelings

Materials Worksheet 2

Either use Worksheet 2 'Relationship Circles' or invite everyone to draw three circles on a piece of card and then colour them in, using coloured pens or crayons, to show three different expressions.

✿ feeling angry

✿ feeling scared

✿ feeling great

Share in the group, and talk about which was the most difficult feeling to draw.

4 Primary Feelings

Materials Worksheets 3–8

Copy the following facial expressions onto cards, enough for each person to have their own set of six faces. These are the six primary feelings, which you can write on the whiteboard before the activity begins:

anger	sorrow or sadness	surprise
joy or happiness	fear	disgust

✿ Discuss if the facial expressions connect with the words.

✿ Decide what colours represent the different feelings, and then colour the expressions.

✿ Develop this activity into using Worksheets 3–8 'Recognising Primary Feelings' in the Resources section. Each worksheet deals with one of the primary feelings.

Moving On

After completing some or all of this section on expressing emotions, people may be ready to move on to Parts 2, 3 and 4. However, it may be that more work needs to be done around emotional literacy first. Worksheets 3–8 'Recognising Primary Feelings', can be used in combination with the Stories & Drama Games found in the Resources section. The three activities that follow are also useful transitions:

✿ Invite participants to bring their own story to a session. This should not be a personal story, but perhaps a story they have created or one they have heard before.

✿ Use movement to express any of the feelings on the Recognising Primary Feelings worksheets; encourage everyone to dance their feelings or paint them on large pieces of paper, or use drumming to express a range of different feelings.

✿ Find poetry that expresses feelings and encourage participants to create their own poems, either through pictures or collage.

Part 2
Embodiment Activities for Emotional Intelligence

The Body is the Emotion

The Body is the Emotion

Working with the body is a means of re-experiencing primary expression; the body is both the container of emotion as well as a means of expressing it. Individual children, who have not had 'good enough' physical holding and containment as babies, usually have difficulties in controlling and contrasting their emotional expression. The exercises in this section are carefully graded in a series of progressions that both 'ground the body' as well as going 'beyond the body'. That is, they assist the child or teenager to live in their body rather than being 'beside themselves' or 'all over the place'. Physical sports are also very helpful for some children, but the competitive nature of most sports does not allow for the repair of primary physical expression.

The Drama & Focus Games in the Resources section are also very physical and can be introduced as additional material in any of the following sessions. Drama games are important for concentration and collaboration, and focus energy that may be diffuse or destructive. For example, when a group struggles with a warm-up exercise, a game such as 'Push Me – Pull You' (p. 105) helps to literally move them on. It is important to encourage participants to bring in their own ideas for games, as emotional intelligence also relies on appropriate responses from others.

The use of the stories and techniques found in the Stories & Storytelling section is a useful way of calming a group that has lost its energy or that needs additional stimulus to the activities. As indicated, stories can be developed in many ways using all of the EPR diversity. The sessions have all been structured to engage the group, develop their ideas and expressions, and to close in a focussed and calm way. The use of individual fleece blankets is deliberate, either as a cushion for those who would not dream of wrapping themselves up, or as a containment and relaxation. Many individuals will progress from one to the other way of using their fleece.

Nevertheless, not everyone is ready to start working physically and it may be that the safety of projective exercises, such as drawing or painting, is the appropriate place to start.

Preparation for Stability & Balance

5

☑ Children ☑ Teenagers

Aims & Focus Introduction of body exercises to develop stability and balance, bearing in mind that many people in the group will feel unstable and out of balance.

Materials Large whiteboard and markers, large drum, fleeces.

Warm Up Bring everyone into a circle, explain the purpose of the group, and invite questions. Allow everyone to run around the room and then 'freeze' several times at the sound of the drum to focus energy. Ask the group to walk around the room, not touching anyone else, and think about their feet making prints on the floor as they move, imagining that they are leaving a trail and keeping their pattern in mind. Then they should retrace their footprints and try to end up where they started. Repeat the walk to drumbeats and move more strongly across the floor really 'making their mark'. Retrace their steps, still to the drumbeat.

Focus Return to the circle and explain the purpose of the group in terms of improving confidence and means of expression, and building physical skills to develop control and balance. Acknowledge the two most important ground rules of keeping yourself and other people safe, which means that no one gets hurt, either physically or verbally. Invite comments and questions and write them on the board.

Activities Resume the warm-up activity and encourage everyone to jump and be aware of their feet leaving and touching the floor each time they jump.

- ✿ With a partner, creep one behind the other. The person following has to stop when their partner stops; swap positions.
- ✿ With a partner, imagine that you are at each end of a see-saw; one stands tall and one bends their knees low, trying to achieve a flow between each other.
- ✿ Hold hands and achieve the same flow, one tall and one low.
- ✿ Repeat the creeping exercise, and use the same foot and pace as your partner; try going forwards and back.
- ✿ Turn it into a funny routine: for example, the person in front turns around and makes their partner jump.

Sharing Show the group the funny routines and discuss what was hard and what was easy. Include ideas from the group for variations on the exercises, perhaps to include next week. Introduce the idea of writing or drawing in journals, or on paper to go in folders. Emphasise that this a private record of their journey through the group, and it will start in the second session (Activity 6 'Shapes & Circles').

Ending Sit back to back with partner on the fleece, close eyes and practise deep breathing.

Embodiment Activities for Emotional Intelligence

6 Shapes & Circles

☑ Children ☑ Teenagers

> **Aims & Focus** To address issues of physical control and body awareness; to develop physical flexibility in order to encourage emotional flexibility; to establish the safety of the circle.

> **Materials** Large whiteboard and markers, large drum, journals or folders, fleeces, Worksheet 1

Warm-up Bring the group into a circle and invite discussion and questions. Acknowledge everyone's name to the beat of the drum: beat the drum and each person says their name; repeat until known! Suggest that the aims of the group and contract can be discussed later; for now, no one should be hurt through actions or words and when the drum gives one loud beat everyone must stop and listen. Invite everyone to walk around the room briskly without any eye contact (light drumbeats); when you bang the drum once, everyone makes a shape that is very tall, very small, very wide, very narrow, very flat, and so on (you could draw the shapes on the board).

Discussion It is important to establish the aims of the group and to agree the ground rules that will form the contract for the time spent together. The aims need to state that the group is about understanding feelings and ways of communicating feelings clearly to others. Mention that there are many ways of communicating feelings: verbally, non-verbally, through pictures and through drama. The ground rules need to emphasise that there will be zero tolerance of any bullying and intimidation, and that everyone's wishes will be respected (see Resources: Worksheet 1 'Contract & Ground Rules for the Group'). Further clarify any important questions.

Activities Return to the shapes from the warm-up exercise and re-state everyone's name.
- ✿ Start in the circle; everyone then runs to the walls and back into the circle again.
- ✿ Imagine that the circle is a prison to break out of before running to the walls and back again.
- ✿ The circle is a thorny hedge to climb over and, yes, there will be lots of 'ows' and 'arghs' while the hedge is climbed!
- ✿ Now swim out of the circle; it becomes harder and harder to swim the closer everyone comes to the walls.
- ✿ Outside of the circle the ground is like a mudslide or bog, and it takes a lot of effort to reach the walls.

> **Sharing** Have the whole group talk about exercises that were fun, silly or boring. Invite suggestions for other games to play next week.

> **Ending** Write or draw in journals or folders, sitting on fleeces.

Reaching for the Sky

✓ Children ✓ Teenagers

Aims & Focus To extend the body beyond its usual limits and to encourage, literally, a feeling of 'reaching out' (and later 'being reached').

Materials Large whiteboard and markers, large drum, soft balls, journals or folders, fleeces, Worksheet 1.

Warm-up Bring everyone into a circle and invite discussion and questions. Repeat the previous exercise (Activity 6: Shapes & Circles) to encourage familiarity with physical work and reinforce the idea that everyone must stop when the drum beats. Invite everyone to run around the room and then jump as high as they can; repeat the jumps until they find their own rhythm.

Discussion Remind group members of the two basic ground rules: that no one is to hurt anyone else, either physically or verbally, and that everyone's wishes will be respected. Invite group members to contribute further suggestions for group rules and write them on the whiteboard. Discuss what is meant by a contract and how it can be agreed by all members of the group, including you. Write ideas on the board (see Worksheet 1 'Contract & Ground Rules for the Group' for further ideas).

Activities Repeat the warm-up of running and jumping to energise the group.

- ✿ Everyone stands still in the circle and reaches for the sky with each arm in turn, then both arms together.
- ✿ Imagine picking apples from a very tall tree and stretching to pick them.
- ✿ With a partner, throw an imaginary ball to each other using very high throws.
- ✿ Use a soft ball and throw it to each other, high across the circle.
- ✿ Partners split up and go into two groups at opposite ends of the room. One group has to wave high to get the attention of their partner in the other group: they could imagine that they are stuck on a rock, in a swamp, or on a roof. The other half of the group then comes to the rescue by guiding their partner to safety across the room, using only gestures.

Sharing Discuss with the whole group what was easy, what was difficult, and what was fun; write the responses on the whiteboard. Invite suggestions for the next meeting.

Ending Write the rescue scene or anything else experienced in journals or folders. Invite everyone to lie down, or sit, on a fleece, and suggest that everyone closes their eyes for five minutes.

Embodiment Activities for Emotional Intelligence

8 Hugging the Circle

☑ Children ☑ Teenagers

Aims & Focus	After the last activity, which concentrated on reaching and 'tallness', this exercise is to work 'wide': in other words, to allow the body to expand in width. Big hugs are the easiest way the achieve this.

Materials	Large whiteboard and markers, large drum, large soft ball, journals or folders, fleeces.

Warm-up   Bring everyone into a circle and invite discussion and questions. Run around the room to fast and slow drumbeats, at first stopping and starting individually, then with a partner. Face your partner and imagine there is a large beach ball between you, so big that your hands cannot join over the top. Carry the imaginary beach ball across the room between you, coordinating your movements with your partner.

Discussion   Check out any issues from previous sessions, address any queries and clarifications; remind the group of the ground rules and contract.

Activities   Continue the ball theme from the warm-up. Throw the soft ball around the group from person to person, then right across the group to the other side, and so on.

- ✿ Pretend to be a giant (or tall *Star Wars* character) and stride around the room with big arm movements.
- ✿ Imagine giving a large, round gift to another giant; in pairs, give and receive huge gifts.
- ✿ Pick up a large discus and throw it in the 'Giant's Olympics'. If the group have suggestions for other Olympic sports, write them on the board and follow on with these.
- ✿ Remind the group that Olympic winners often get hugged; practise how the giants will hug, if necessary with no actual touching.
- ✿ Introduce the idea of hugging the world, or a huge tree, or the president of Giantland!

Sharing	Allow time for everyone to return to their own size again, and talk about how it felt to be larger than life. Who is more scary, a large silent person or a small sarcastic person?

Ending	Write or draw in journals or folders while sitting on fleeces; relax back to back with a partner and repeat some deep breaths.

Star Shapes & Jumps

☑ Children ☑ Teenagers

Aims & Focus	To progress from the 'tall' and 'wide' positions of the previous two activities to star shapes that can open the body further, help balance, and allow energy to be freed.

Materials	Large whiteboard and markers, large drum, journals or folders, fleeces.

Warm-up   Bring everyone into a seated circle and invite feedback or questions. Ask everyone to do star jumps on the spot, with arms outstretched on the diagonal and legs wide, so that both arms and legs form a V. Once they are comfortable with this, ask them to open their legs with the jump and then close them again, like scissors, when they land. Experiment with jumps that go from leg to leg when you land. Use the drumbeat to mark the rhythm of the jumps.

Discussion   Feedback from previous session and any questions or suggestions. Explain that the different movements free up different parts of the body, and that the development of breathing exercises allows the lungs to expand and carry oxygen to different body parts.

Activities   Invite everyone to lie flat on the floor in the star position and try to take up as much floor space as possible.

✿ Remind everyone of the way that their bodies expanded when they were pretending to be giants, and encourage more expansion to make a big star.

✿ Roll onto one side of the body and curl up with hands around your knees; practise opening wide to be a star and then curling up into a ball again.

✿ Breathe in when becoming the star and blow the air through the mouth when contracting into the ball.

✿ Lie in a comfortable position, place a hand on the diaphragm and feel it move as you breathe in and out: in through the nose, and out through the mouth.

✿ Experiment with deep breathing as everyone lies in the star position.

Sharing	Invite the group to come into a sitting position and share how they feel: explain in simple terms why the deep breathing is so important (see Resources: Breathing Exercises, p. 113).

Ending	Write or draw in journals or folders, while sitting on fleeces.

10 Breathing the Dragon

 ✓ Children ◯ Teenagers

> **Aims & Focus** To encourage healthy breathing and expand the potential of the voice and its range.

> **Materials** Large whiteboard and markers, journals or folders, mats or fleeces.

Warm-up Bring everyone into a circle and invite discussion and questions. Walk like dragons around the room, big steps and big claws, big breaths blowing out fire. Freeze and look around, then walk again as a very angry dragon, still breathing fire. Walk as a small dragon with just a little bit of fire. Write the main points of the contract you have agreed on the whiteboard.

Discussion Feedback and comments; questions and suggestions. Explain that dragon exercises will help with breathing, and that people should listen carefully to instructions, because sometimes the dragon will be angry and sometimes it will be expressing a different emotion.

Activities Invite everyone to lie down on a mat or fleece and breathe deeply.

✿ Suggest to everyone that they are the dragon lying down and resting, but that they are still breathing fire, which is normal dragon behaviour. Perhaps dragon breathing is quite noisy!

✿ As they are resting, ask everyone to think about what dragons might be scared of? How would they breathe if they were scared?

✿ Invite the group to stand and stretch, putting mats or fleeces to one side. Divide into two groups, with one group walking around the room as angry dragons and the other as scared dragons.

✿ In pairs, through sounds and movements, pretend that a scared dragon is interacting with an angry dragon; then change roles.

✿ Create a story in the pairs about how the angry dragon is scared of something, and the frightened dragon helps him or her to overcome their fear (this is expanded in Part 4: Role Sessions, Activities 30 & 31).

> **Sharing** Each pair can share their story by telling it together to the whole group.

> **Ending** Write or draw in journals or folders. Relax, sitting or lying on the floor on fleeces.

More Breath – More Voice!

☐ Children ☑ Teenagers

Aims & Focus To increase awareness of the importance of developing the breathing capacity. Deep breathing helps people to replenish the oxygen in their blood-streams, which is important for health and energy levels. Voices will increase in power and people feel more energised when they have more oxygen in their bloodstreams. This exercise can be a means of increasing well-being as well as serving as a basis for emotional expression.

Materials Large whiteboard and markers, large paper bags, journals or folders, fleeces.

Warm-up Bring everyone into a circle for discussion and questions. Ask everyone to run round the room and experiment with the difference between breath needed for a short sprint and that needed for a long race: the former needs quick intakes and the latter needs sustained breathing to last the pace. Experiment with different in-breaths (for surprise, shock, fear and excitement), out-breaths (for sighs, pleasure, relief and disappointment), the holding of breath (for sorrow, depression and fear) and an explosion of breath (in anger and irritability).

Discussion Share any new ideas. Explain that the focus is on the breath because it supports energy, and the way in which different types of breath are needed for different situations. Write any new ideas on the board.

Activities Give everyone the opportunity to test the different types of breathing by indicating a mood or a feeling to which the group responds. Improvise the following scenes as people move around the room and freeze:

- ✿ Work as individuals. Turning a corner you see a large car crash: react with shock, then fear because you may know the driver, then relief when you realise you do not.
- ✿ Open a large parcel that you think it is something you really want, but turns out to be something for someone else. Respond with excitement, then disappointment, then irritation.
- ✿ See someone in the distance that you think you know well, sprint towards them, then stop short when you realise it is someone else. React with excitement, disbelief and finally disappointment.
- ✿ Blow up a paper bag and make it bang as loudly as possible.
- ✿ In small groups create a simple scene in which the paper bag noise becomes crucial to the story that is being enacted.

Sharing Share how it felt when expressing the different feelings; tell the story with the paper bag noise; share the stories from each group.

Ending Write or draw in journals or folders; relax back to back with partner.

Embodiment Activities for Emotional Intelligence

12 Creating the Feelings Map 1

 Children Teenagers

> **Aims & Focus** To create a learning session during which it is understand that there is a need for emotions to be able to coexist, without one wiping out another. For example, it is possible to feel very angry and also very sad.

> **Materials** Large whiteboard and markers, large drum, journals or folders, fleeces.

Warm-up Bring everyone into a circle for discussion and questions. Introduce the idea that feelings can coexist, and that just because one is angry that anger does not have to overwhelm other feelings. Invite everyone to form pairs and to number themselves One or Two in their pairs. Everyone runs around the room until the drumbeat sounds and you call out 'Ones are angry'. All of the Ones then have to make an angry face or body-sculpt anger, after which the Twos express the opposite emotion (see Resources: Body Sculpting). Repeat with several feelings, alternating between the Ones and Twos miming the initial feeling.

Discussion How did it feel to experience two opposite feelings at the same time? Could you experience three feelings at the same time? Which are the most difficult feelings that overwhelm all the others?

Activities Introduce the idea of a feelings map that can be shown with body sculpts and movement:

- ✿ Draw a map on the whiteboard, divide it into six areas, and write the six primary feelings (fear, joy, anger, sadness, disgust, surprise) in the spaces. Invite group members to choose colours to represent the feelings and to colour in the spaces.
- ✿ Everyone recreates the map in the room by body-sculpting the feelings (divide the group into six small groups and allocate a feeling that each group has to enact).
- ✿ On the drumbeat the groups express their feeling through movement.
- ✿ On the drumbeat the groups express their feeling through sound.
- ✿ On the drumbeat the groups express their feelings through sound and movement (allow each groups to express the range of feelings).

> **Sharing** Stay in the small groups and talk about how it felt, and which was the easiest part of the map.

> **Ending** Allow plenty of relaxation time with fleeces, and write in journals or folders.

 ℗ This page may be photocopied for instructional use only. *Creative Activities for Developing Emotional Intelligence* © Sue Jennings 2013

Telling the Story 1

☑ Children   ☑ Teenagers

Aims & Focus To bring together the sequencing of feelings in a simple narrative that does not need words. To recognise feelings that are expressed non-verbally.

Materials Large whiteboard and markers, large drum, journals or folders, fleeces.

Warm-up Bring everyone into a circle for discussion and questions. It is important to acknowledge people's progress and to agree that many of the exercises are difficult. Suggest that everyone walks around the room with a simple story in their head that they saw on TV, whether on the news or in a soap opera. Allow them to use the walking time to remember it. Then enact the story with gestures and movements, exaggerating the movements as much as possible. Indicate the beginning and end with a drumbeat. Write any feelings on the whiteboard.

Discussion How people use their movements and gestures when they are telling stories: 'the human body is never still'. Suggest they try turning the TV sound down to test whether they can still understand the story through the movements.

Activities Invite the group to create pairs and to choose one of their stories, combine the stories, or to choose a new one.

- ✿ Each pair tells their story together, using very exaggerated movements (as in the warm-up).
- ✿ Tell the story again, using just one finger and facial expressions.
- ✿ Repeat the story (add to it, if wished) as if it was a murder mystery, with ordinary movements.
- ✿ Choose another way to tell the story (e.g., as a period drama, sci-fi, or as if told by cave people).
- ✿ Each pair repeats the style they liked best for the whole group.

Sharing As a group, discuss the different styles of narrative that still allowed everyone to express their emotions.

Ending Write or draw in journals or folders and then relax, wrapped in the fleeces.

Embodiment Activities for Emotional Intelligence

14 Telling the Story 2

☑ Children ☑ Teenagers

Aims & Focus To bring together a clear story structure that contains the feelings of each character and allows for recognition of those feelings.

Materials Large whiteboard and markers, large drum, journals or folders, fleeces.

Warm-up Bring everyone into a circle for discussion and questions. Ask everyone to run around the room, shake out their arms and legs, and do a few leaps in the air to drumbeats. Each individual expresses an emotion on the drumbeat, quickly followed by another: for example, you could call out 'surprise', then 'sadness', until a range of feelings have been expressed.

Discussion How difficult is it for other people to recognise how we feel, and for us to recognise what other people are feeling? Write on the board the feelings people think are most difficult to recognise.

Activities Everyone works in pairs and the theme is 'misunderstood feelings'.

- ✿ One person expresses a feeling, while their partner deliberately mimes a different feeling.
- ✿ One person mimes a feeling, the other person a different one, and then the first person enacts their feeling even more forcefully.
- ✿ Invite each pair to create a simple story that involves mistaken feelings: e.g., someone comforts another person because they think they are crying, but in reality it is a cold!
- ✿ Everyone develops a short story that could have serious consequences if the expression of emotion was misunderstood (e.g., someone trying to explain that there is a fire, and the other person thinking they are asking for directions!)
- ✿ Each pair enacts their favourite story for the whole group.

Sharing Talk about when non-verbal communication is more difficult and whether it is over-used or under-used.

Ending Write or draw in journals or folders. Long relaxation with fleeces.

Part 3
Projective Activities for Emotional Intelligence

The Picture is the Story

The Picture is the Story

The sessions and activities that focus on projective techniques through drawing, painting and collage mirror the early developmental stage when infants go beyond their own bodies and relate to objects and substances that are 'out there'. Although many experiences are very sensory (such as using finger paints or working in a 'messy space') and therefore could be called embodiment, they are also beyond the body and combine the categories of embodiment and projection. Projective activities enable participants to give form to feelings in a way that is both visible and tangible. Whereas embodiment activities are over when the movement has stopped, apart from any sensations there may be in the body, projective creations allow something to be kept and reflected on, and encourage 'staying with' a picture or model.

Drama games and stories (see Resources) can also be integrated into these sessions as a means of expanding a subject or focussing energy. Many individuals have difficulty in managing the actual amount of emotion to express; they almost require a new 'recipe', whose ingredients are more carefully measured!

It is very important to establish the intellectual property of the drawings and other art objects. They belong to the person (or the group) who created them and ultimately that person can take them away. It is for the whole group to decide what they wish to be done with a group painting, for example.

Preparation for Stability & Balance

☑ Children ☑ Teenagers

Aims & Focus The introduction of drawing and modelling exercises to develop stability and balance, bearing in mind that many people in the group will feel unstable and out of balance.

Materials Large whiteboard and markers, large pieces of drawing/sugar paper or card, large crayons or coloured markers, journals or folders, fleeces, copies of Worksheet 9 'Foot Template'.

Warm-up Bring everyone into a circle and invite discussion and questions. Invite the group to walk around the room, not touching anyone else, and to think about their feet making prints on the floor as they move; they should imagine that they are leaving a trail and keep that pattern in mind, as well as the shape of their feet as they walk. Repeat, walking and making their footprints more strongly.

Discussion Remind everyone of the two most important ground rules: that everyone keeps themselves and other people safe (which means that no one gets hurt, either physically or verbally), and each person's wishes are respected. Describe how the drawing/sticking/painting exercises that follow build on the physical work they have already done.

Activities Resume from the warm-up and encourage everyone to jump and to be aware of their feet leaving and touching the floor each time they jump. In pairs, invite everyone to stand on the large pieces of paper while their partner draws around their feet (people should feel free to stand how they wish – with feet together, one in front of the other, and so on). Otherwise use the foot template on Worksheet 9.

✿ Colour in the foot outlines and put in any extra detail that people may wish to add.

✿ Think of any expressions about feet and write them around the edge of the paper (e.g., wrong-footed, best foot forward; see the detailed list on Worksheet 9).

✿ Write any expressions about feet on the board.

✿ Invite the group to think about 'planting your feet firmly on the ground'.

✿ Suggest that people can add things to their picture so their feet look firmer.

Sharing Share pictures with partners and any thoughts about stability versus instability.

Ending Write or draw in journals or folders, then sit back to back with partner on fleece and practise deep breathing.

Projective Activities for Emotional Intelligence

16 Shapes & Circles

☑ Children ☑ Teenagers

Aims & Focus To further develop the 'safety of the circle' and create circles and spikes that can be turned into something else.

Materials Large whiteboard and markers, large crayons and coloured pens, Worksheets 2 'Relationship Circles' and 10 'Spiky & Jagged Feelings' (at least two of each for each person), journals or folders, fleeces.

Warm-up Bring everyone together into a seated circle, acknowledge everyone's name again, and invite discussion and questions. Encourage everyone to run around the room and make circle shapes and spiky shapes.

Discussion Remind everyone of the contract and why the group exists; to help people to express their feelings so that they can be better understood. Drawing is one way to achieve this, however, this is not an art class as such, and no one is expected to do things they are not ready for.

Activities Return to the warm-up and invite half the group to make 'circle arms' and the other half to make 'spiky fingers'; if circles manage to catch spikes and encircle them, then spikes turn into circles. The aim is for the whole group to become circles.

🌞 Everyone has their own Worksheet 10 to colour in and then to try to turn the shape into something else (e.g., a fire, someone's spiky hair).

🌞 Each person can use another spiky worksheet and turn it into feelings by colouring in and extending the idea (e.g., someone feels 'prickly').

🌞 Using their own Worksheet 2, create a very strong outline in a favourite colour and then put colours and shapes for positive feelings inside.

🌞 Experiment to see if it is possible to put the spiky worksheet inside the circle worksheet by cutting or redrawing.

Sharing Within the whole group talk about reactions to the circles and spikes, and share important words and feelings.

Ending Write or draw in journals or folders; relax back to back, sitting on fleeces.

Reaching for the Sky   17

☑ Children ☑ Teenagers

Aims & Focus To project beyond people's immediate perceptions; to practise 'reaching out' and 'reaching up' (and later 'being reached').

Materials Large whiteboard and coloured markers, Worksheet 11 'Stars' (one for each person), crayons, journals or folders, fleeces.

Warm-up Bring everyone into a circle and invite discussion and questions. Invite everyone to run around the room and then jump as high as they can, repeating the jumps until they find their own rhythm. Practise the footprint walking again (Activity 15 Preparation for Stability & Balance) with everyone placing feet firmly on the ground.

Discussion Remind group members of the two basic ground rules: no one is to hurt anyone else, either physically or verbally, and each person's wishes should be respected. Discuss the idea of reaching out or reaching up; what would that feel like? Accept ideas and suggestions and write them on the board.

Activities Repeat the warm-up of running and jumping, and then change it to running and reaching out, and running and reaching up.

✿ Use Worksheet 11 and colour each star in a favourite colour

✿ Write down any words or phrases or songs that mention stars; for example, 'Catch a Falling Star and Put it in Your Pocket', 'Star Wars', 'Stars in Your Eyes'.

✿ Invite everyone to draw a character from *Star Wars*, with a focus on the feelings, not the fighting.

✿ Write down the feelings this character has, and how they express them

✿ Draw several circles around the character and write or draw a feeling in each one.

Sharing Discuss with the whole group what was easy, what was difficult, what was fun, and write the responses on the whiteboard. Invite suggestions for the next meeting. Share the similarities and differences of all the *Star Wars* characters.

Ending Write or draw in journals or folders. Invite everyone to lie or sit on a fleece and think about starring in a film – what would the film be called?

Projective Activities for Emotional Intelligence

18 Circles to Hug & Circles to Change

☑ Children ☑ Teenagers

Aims & Focus To explore different ways of containing feelings and expressing them appropriately; to practise new responses to old stimuli.

Materials Large whiteboard and markers, Worksheet 2 'Relationship Circles' (two for each person), large drum, large soft ball, journals or folders, fleeces.

Warm-up Bring the group into a circle and invite discussion and questions. Run around the room to fast and slow drumbeats; throw the large soft ball to each other, but try not to catch it. The winner is the person who does not touch the ball! Repeat several times until the 'catch' response has stopped. Then change the game, saying that you will call out a number and that is the number of people who should attempt to catch the ball; use a variety of numbers until the whole group has a chance to catch the ball.

Discussion Remind the group, if necessary, about the ground rules and contract. Talk about the difference between competitive sports and non-competitive sports or New Games. Share how some people like hugging and others do not.

Activities Continue the ball theme from the warm-up; allow group members to throw the ball high while calling out the number of people to catch it.

✿ Using Worksheet 2, invite everyone to colour in different circles.

✿ Draw different expressions in each circle as if they were faces.

✿ Use a second Worksheet 2 and give the circles arms, reaching in different directions; what are the fingers like? Experiment by drawing the circles hugging each other.

✿ Draw the hug you would like to have and write on it who would hug you.

Sharing Share the two finished worksheets with a partner and talk about how it felt to draw them.

Ending Write or draw in journals or folders; sit back to back with partner and think about the hug theme.

Feet on the Ground & Stars in the Sky

✓ Children ✓ Teenagers

Aims & Focus For participants to progress to feeling secure and balanced 'on the ground', and to reach out to the stars with some confidence.

Materials Large whiteboard and markers, foot template on Worksheet 9, Worksheet 12 'Carpet of Stars' (one of each for each person), A4 paper, crayons and coloured pens, journals or folders, fleeces, Story Sheet 1, 'Star Woman'

Warm-up Bring everyone into a circle and invite discussion and questions. Encourage people to run around the room and then freeze, either in a star shape (stretching up), or in a foot shape (crouching low). Call out 'star' or 'feet', so that people respond accordingly.

Discussion Suggest that security is achieved by having our feet on the ground, but reaching for the stars at the same time. Perhaps this helps us to find the 'balance between the earth and the sky', with our spine acting like the trunk of a tree? Write other ideas from the group on the board.

Activities If necessary repeat the warm-up exercise above.

✿ Invite everyone to use copies of the foot template on Worksheet 9 to create their own paths and patterns across the floor and then follow them as if they were a track (be aware that if people actually tread on the paper footprints they may slip depending on your floor surface).

✿ Using Worksheet 12, suggest that everyone can colour the very deep blue of the sky and the bright yellow of the stars. For older members, suggest that this is an illustration for a story called 'Star Woman' (see Resources: Stories & Storytelling, Story Sheet 1), or their own star story.

✿ In groups of three or four, create a joint picture that includes both footprints and stars; what is going on in between?

✿ Decide on a title for the picture in the group and agree it together.

✿ Discuss if the picture tells a story and what might it be?

Sharing Invite the smaller groups to come back into the large group with their picture and tell everyone the titles they chose.

Ending Write or draw in journals or folders; relax on, or under, fleeces.

Projective Activities for Emotional Intelligence

20 The Dragon's Footprints

☑ Children   ◯ Teenagers

Aims & Focus Expanding ideas and feelings and how they can be expressed.

Materials Large whiteboard and markers, A3 or A4 drawing paper, pencils, acrylic paints and brushes (including gold paint), journals or folders, fleeces.

Warm-up Bring everyone into a circle and invite discussion and questions. Walk like dragons around the room, with big steps and big claws, focus on big footprints; then stretch out enormous wings and take off and fly; come to rest again.

Discussion Encourage suggestions for activities on the theme of dragons and write them on the board. Incorporate them where appropriate. Explain that dragons have special tails to help them balance when they fly.

Activities Invite everyone to close their eyes and imagine a dragon of their choice – what colour is it? Dragons almost always have some gold in their colouring.

- ✿ Suggest to everyone that they paint the dragon they can see in their heads.
- ✿ Sketch it first and then paint it with big brush strokes (smaller children will need larger sheets of paper).
- ✿ Try to let the picture fill up the paper as much as possible.
- ✿ Write the words for the dragon's feelings (happy, angry, etc.) on the edge of the paper, and write or paint the dragon' name.
- ✿ Now draw another dragon that is sleeping: how is this one feeling?

Sharing Show the dragon pictures and words to the group.

Ending Write or draw in journals or folders; wrap up in fleeces and relax back to back with a partner.

The Dragon T-Shirt

 Children ☑ Teenagers

Aims & Focus To encourage creating ideas from other ideas; to think about the way in which initial feelings can lead into creative work.

Materials Large whiteboard and markers, various sizes of paper and coloured pens or acrylic paints, bright colours (including silver and gold), pencils and sharpener, examples of T-shirt design (Worksheet 13, 'Dragon T-shirt template', or a blank T-shirt template), journals or folders, fleeces, Worksheet 2 for circle templates.

Warm-up Bring everyone into a circle and invite discussion and questions. Suggest that they all have a good stretch, do some deep breathing and focus their minds on the idea of design.

Discussion Introduce the idea of a T-shirt design that is very specific: a fire-breathing dragon with claws, tail and, of course, wings. Encourage discussion of logos, emblems and badges. Discuss the idea that badges and emblems help us to state who we are.

Activities Have a quick stretch and shake-out of fingers in preparation for holding things, big yawn and then settle.

✿ Draw circles for making badges (or use Worksheet 2 'Relationship Circles').

✿ Create faces with different expressions on the badges.

✿ Create a dragon that is suitable to go on a T-shirt.

✿ What does it express, this dragon? Strong feelings?

✿ Paint blocks of strong colour that would be easy to print on a real T-shirt.

Sharing Put all of the dragon pictures on the wall and look at similarities and differences.

Ending Write or draw in journals or folders. Relax on, or under, a fleece.

Projective Activities for Emotional Intelligence

22 Creating the Feelings Map 2

☑ Children ☑ Teenagers

Projective Activities for Emotional Intelligence

> **Aims & Focus** Integrating contrasting feelings in one space and allowing different feelings to be a part of the whole.

> **Materials** Large whiteboard and markers, A4 paper, coloured pens or crayons, Worksheet 14 'A Feelings Map', journals or folders, fleeces.

Warm-up Bring everyone together in a seated circle for discussion and questions. Explore the idea of why we have maps and what they can illustrate. Encourage everyone to run around the room and freeze when a feeling word is called out, then to use their entire body to express the feeling as strongly as possible.

Discussion Discuss the ways in which the feelings they expressed with their bodies can be shown through drawing or colouring, and introduce the idea of different feelings having different colours. Why do traffic lights use green and red?

Activities Using Worksheet 14 'A Feelings Map', draw a map on the whiteboard and suggest possibilities for colouring in our personal map of feelings (try Worksheets 15 'A Feelings Heart' or 16 'A Feelings Rainbow' for younger children).

🔆 Invite everyone to draw a bold outline of a map that fills the page.

🔆 Divide up the map with lines to suggest different areas of feelings.

🔆 Choose colours to represent different feelings and colour in the areas for each feeling on the map.

🔆 Draw a colour code at the bottom to indicate which colour is for which feeling.

🔆 Look at the different sizes of the sections on the map and reflect which is the biggest and which is the smallest.

> **Sharing** With a partner, compare and talk about your maps and how it felt to make them.

> **Ending** Write or draw in journals or folders; relax back to back with partner on, or under, a fleece.

Drawing the Story 1

☑ Children ☑ Teenagers

Aims & Focus To assist individuals to create characters who express feelings by using cartoon-style drawing and paper and pen games.

Materials Large whiteboard, examples of exaggerated expressions from magazines or comics, cartoons of famous people, A4 paper, coloured pens, journals or folders, fleeces.

Warm-up Bring everyone together in a seated circle for discussion and questions. Introduce the idea of exaggeration and how feelings can be expressed in an 'over-the-top' way. Invite the group to walk around the room and freeze in exaggerated poses that mimic activities involving strong feelings: for example, 'giving', 'taking', 'building', 'knocking down', 'winning', 'losing', and so on.

Discussion Explore the idea of exaggerated facial expressions, and the way in which artists can evoke the essence of a person by using them. If the group is young, see if they recognise cartoons of famous people.

Activities Using A4 paper and crayons or pens, individuals can try the following:

✿ Draw a large face with exaggerated features and expression.

✿ Name the feeling the face is expressing.

✿ Try and copy the feeling with a facial expression of your own (lots of giggles and laughter here).

✿ Use sheets of A5 paper and an adaptation of the game of 'Consequences'. Everyone sits in a circle and each person draws a hat on their paper, folds it over, and passes it on. The next person draws a face and passes it on. Each person in turn adds an element (body, arms, legs, etc.), until the picture arrives back at the person before the one who originally drew the hat. The last person then writes the feeling that the picture expresses and completes the phrase, 'And then I shouted ...!'

✿ Everyone unfolds the drawing that they started themselves and looks at the character: what they are feeling and what they shouted.

Sharing In the whole group, look at the pictures and feelings, keeping it light-hearted and fun.

Ending Write or draw in journals or folders, then relax and do deep breathing on, or under, fleeces. If there is giggling, encourage it and then calm it down.

Projective Activities for Emotional Intelligence

24 Drawing the Story 2

☑ Children ☑ Teenagers

Aims & Focus Developing the ability to create narrative that conveys contrasting feelings and in which there is a positive resolution to conflict.

Materials Large whiteboard and markers, examples of cartoons from comics, magazines and newspapers (matched to ages), A4 paper, crayons or coloured pens, journals or folders, fleeces.

Warm-up Bring everyone into a seated circle for discussion and questions. Introduce the idea of cartoons and the way they use exaggeration: for example, hair standing on end, distorted facial expressions. Invite the group to walk around the room and then to freeze in a cartoon expression when you call out 'fright', 'shock', 'fantastic', 'wow', and so on.

Discussion Elaborate the idea of cartoons and what they communicate. Show examples from comics and newspapers; compose a cartoon with the group, drawing it on the whiteboard.

Activities Give the group a choice between drawing their own cartoon and cutting out pictures from magazines and comics in order to create a cartoon sequence.

- ✿ Divide a sheet of A4 paper into six sections or boxes. (Use the whiteboard to illustrate.)
- ✿ In box 1 draw or stick a picture of who is in this cartoon story (who?).
- ✿ In boxes 2 and 3 add what are they doing and where (what? and where?).
- ✿ In box 4 the character has a surprise or a shock (who? and what?).
- ✿ In box 5 and 6, say how are they feeling and how it ends (how?).

Sharing Share all the stories with the whole group and comment on what the characters are feeling.

Ending Write or draw in journals or folders; relax on, or under, fleeces.

Part 4
Role Activities for Emotional Intelligence

The Drama is the Knowledge

The Drama is the Knowledge

The role section provides carefully graded exercises in order for participants to reflect on their own behaviour and feelings by 'playing themselves' in short dramas. Many children and young people will go through life in a reactive and predictable way. There is never 'pause for thought' (Jennings, 2011a), or time to consider how another person might be feeling, because empathy has not developed. In role work participants are able to develop and differentiate between 'everyday reality' and 'dramatic reality', which is the reality of 'let's pretend' (Jennings, 1990). The first act of 'let's pretend' occurs when a newborn baby tries to imitate the expression on his or her mother's face; the whole of the first year of life is a series of evolving drama games between the adult and infant. Eventually the baby is able to grasp 'me and not me', and to strengthen their own identity through an awareness of others.

I suggest that 'the drama is the knowledge', because it is the only means of developing both an understanding of self and other. Many people shy away from drama, both children and adults, because they have felt silly or exposed in badly handled role-play exercises. The use of drama games and dramatised stories is an excellent and reassuring means of developing confidence in the drama. It could be said that with the confidence to do drama, drama will build all the confidence that anyone needs!

Always allow time for coming out of role after engaging with any sort of drama activity; people need time to 'become themselves again', to 'de-role' from dramatic reality back to everyday.

Stability & Balance

25

☑ Children ☑ Teenagers

Aims & Focus To create a feeling of security in the group and awareness of appropriate expressions in role play.

Materials Large whiteboard and markers, journals or folders, fleeces, Worksheet 9.

Warm-up Bring everyone into a seated circle and invite feedback or questions. Explain that the themes explored previously will now be explored through role play and drama. Invite the group members to walk briskly around the room; call out 'freeze' and then a word describing a mood or attitude, for example: 'impatient', 'tired', 'frustrated', 'bored', 'fed-up', 'pleased', 'cool', and so on. Everyone then walks on, dramatising that mood until the next freeze. Ask the group to contribute their own suggestions and write all the mood words on the whiteboard.

Discussion If necessary remind the group of the ground rules, and add a new rule that in role play and drama swearing and cursing is not permitted. If an individual character in a drama is someone who swears, then this can be discussed in the group first.

Activities Following on from the activities in the previous sections (Preparation for Stability & Balance in Part 2: Embodiment Sessions and Part 3: Projective Sessions), look at the list of foot expressions on Worksheet 9 and choose two or three to develop as roles, for instance: 'stand your ground'; 'feet don't touch the ground'; and 'put your foot down'. If you choose 'stand your ground' (for example), the group can first discuss the idea and then develop it:

✿ Everyone stands in the posture of a person who 'stands their ground'.

✿ With a partner discuss what sort of person needs to 'stand their ground'.

✿ Create a situation in which one person needs to 'stand their ground' against someone else who is trying to persuade them to do something they don't want.

✿ Change around so that everyone has a turn at 'standing their ground', but vary the reasons.

✿ Demonstrate brief role plays to the group.

Sharing Discuss situations which are familiar, and whether 'standing your ground' has difficulties.

Ending Write or draw in journals or folders; relax on, or under, fleeces, close eyes and be mindful of any feelings experienced during the role plays.

Role Activities for Emotional Intelligence

26 Shapes & Circles

 ✓ Children ✓ Teenagers

Aims & Focus To encourage participants to make connections between their body posture (shapes) and gestures, the emotions they may be feeling, and the reactions from others.

Materials Large whiteboard and markers, journals or folders, fleeces.

Warm-up Bring everyone into a seated circle and invite feedback and questions. Explain the connections between body posture and feelings, and how some physical gestures can give the wrong impression or provoke another person. Stand up, shake out limbs and run around the room in preparation for creating 'freeze shapes' with different gestures, such as a friendly wave, closed fist, high-five, pushing someone else, blocking your ears, and so on.

Discussion Talk about whether certain gestures happen without us being aware of them, how they make us feel, and their effect on others.

Activities Give the group a theme for a role play in pairs, such as 'That scares me', or 'That makes me angry'. However, the role plays should start with a physical gesture, as practised in the warm-up. In pairs:

✿ Discuss which gesture to use to start role play.

✿ Decide who the two characters are, their ages, if they know each other.

✿ Explore a situation where they meet.

✿ Experience the 'being scared' or 'being angry'.

✿ Experiment and change the role play for a different outcome.

Sharing Discuss in the group the gestures and roles, and whether participants were able to change a situation and its outcome.

Ending Write or draw in journals or folders. On fleeces, sit back to back with partner and reflect on any changes of feelings and gestures.

Role Activities for Emotional Intelligence

Reaching for the Sky

✓ Children ✓ Teenagers

Aims & Focus To support young people to go 'beyond themselves' and recognise the limitations imposed by others.

Materials Large whiteboard and markers, hats and caps (for a chef, surgeon, nurse, baseball cap, tennis headband, etc.), journals or folders, fleeces.

Warm-up Bring everyone into a seated circle and invite feedback and questions. Explain that sometimes we are limited by our view of ourselves, but more often by the views of others. Invite the group members to share some typical phrases, such as 'You'll never make a go if it', or 'You'll always end up at the bottom of the pile', and write them on the board. Energise the group by inviting everyone to run around the room, shouting out 'I can and I will'.

Discussion Suggest that group members choose a 'put-down' phrase that is relevant to them and discuss what the opposite would be; so if someone is 'bottom of the pile', how would it feel to be 'top of the pile'?

Activities Expanding on the theme of 'I can and I will', invite everyone to choose a hat or cap that indicates a role they have not thought about before.

- ✿ Walk around the room wearing the hat and absorbing how that person is: their confidence, skills, how other people see them.

- ✿ In pairs, stay in role and talk about your work and your success: maybe two surgeons are discussing an operation, a chef is describing a new dish to a tennis player.

- ✿ Change pairs and now share a disaster: the operation that failed, the dish that collapsed, or the missed goals.

- ✿ Remove the hat, shake off the role, and now be 'in role' as yourself, sharing the experience of a disaster or getting something wrong.

- ✿ Stay as yourself and share a success, an achievement, and a goal to aim for in the future.

Sharing In the whole group compare feelings of success and failure, and how to strengthen the feelings of success.

Ending Write or draw in journals or folders. Relax wrapped up in a fleece, and 'breathe in' the possibility of change.

Role Activities for Emotional Intelligence

28 Hugging Who?

 ☑ Children ☑ Teenagers

Aims & Focus To establish appropriate boundaries for touch, and a feeling of 'reaching out' and 'being reached'.

Materials Large whiteboard and markers, Worksheet 2 'Relationship Circles', journals or folders, fleeces.

Warm-up Bring everyone into a seated circle and invite feedback and questions. Introduce the themes of hugging, touching, not touching, already explored in earlier sections. Everyone walks around the room, at first keeping as far as possible away from others, then closer but not touching, then closer still and touching shoulders lightly as they pass.

Discussion The importance of touch as a clear signal to another person, and that full-frontal hugs are only appropriate with close family. Movements can be perceived as threatening, or too intimate, or rejecting. Draw on the board one circle in the centre, a circle of circles around it, and another circle of circles outside; share ideas of intimacy and distance (use Worksheet 2).

Activities The following role plays happen with no physical touch – any touch should be indicated or implied through gestures.

✿ In pairs, stand an 'arm's length' from each other and discuss if this feels 'comfortable' or OK for talking to each other. One person takes a step forward; does it still feel OK?

✿ Take the same position and one person takes a step back; how is communication now?

✿ Stay at 'arm's length' and create a scene where someone is very upset, for example their pet has died; do they want to move closer?

✿ Stay at 'arm's length' and one person criticises the other; do they want to move further away?

✿ Create a scene in small groups where someone is rejected by their friends; how will they get back into their group?

Sharing Discuss with the whole group what was easy, what was difficult, and what was fun; write the responses on the whiteboard and invite suggestions for the next meeting.

Ending Write or draw in journals or folders. Invite everyone to lie down or sit on the floor (they can have a fleece if they wish), and suggest everyone closes their eyes for five minutes.

Role Activities for Emotional Intelligence

Being a Star

29

 Children  Teenagers

Aims & Focus To internalise feelings of success and recognition in order to build confidence and self-esteem.

Materials Large whiteboard and markers, pieces of material and hats for role-playing, Worksheet 11 'Stars' (one for each person), journals or folders, fleeces.

Warm-up Bring everyone into a seated circle and invite feedback and questions. Remind people of the 'star work' they have done before, and that this session is about feeling like a star, for themselves. Walk briskly around the room, then call 'freeze' and everyone makes a star shape. Repeat and make the shape with a partner, then with three people, slowly increasing the numbers until finally you try to make a star shape with everyone in the group.

Discussion Why are we given (or not given) stars for our school work? How does it make us feel? Encourage people to supply examples of competitiveness, for example on TV programmes where someone has to be the winner. How does it feel not to be the winner or to feel 'second best'.

Activities The following role play can be done in pairs or small groups; the groups themselves can decide which characters should be involved in the drama. Each story has a basic plot – but there are a range of potential outcomes. Develop the idea that the responses will change with the individuals – there is no 'right' answer. Materials and hats can be used to enhance roles.

✪ A prince (princess) has been told by the King's assistant that a new star has been named after him (or her). The reaction is: 'What! I am just one amongst millions, how dare you!'

✪ The same scene, but this time the response is: 'Are you sure? There must be some mistake, my father would not name a star after me; it must be someone else.'

✪ The same scene, but this time the response is: 'That is wonderful, I can hardly believe it! A star – after me! Wow!'

✪ Create a scene where the first or second response has been reported back to the King and he asks to see the prince (princess). Explore what the conversation could be about.

✪ Using Worksheet 11 (the second page, with several stars on it), write or draw in each star something that you are good at, at school or outside.

Sharing Share the thoughts and feelings about the role play in the whole group, including what was easy and what was more difficult.

Ending Write or draw in journals or folders; on fleeces, relax back to back with a partner, eyes closed.

Role Activities for Emotional Intelligence

☑ Children ⬤ Teenagers

Role Activities for Emotional Intelligence

> **Aims & Focus** To build on the previous dragon work to develop inner strength and confidence; to integrate the physical with the vocal and the emotional with the behavioural; and to encourage turn-taking and sharing between members.

> **Materials** Large whiteboard with markers, large pieces of material, journals or folders, fleeces. For dragon masks: A5 pieces of card, coloured markers, elastic.

Warm-up Bring everyone into a seated circle and invite feedback and questions. Introduce the idea of creating plays about dragons. Run around the room individually and freeze as a dragon. Suggest that two people can make a dragon together. Everyone runs around the room in pairs that freeze as one dragon; then they walk around the room together with large footprints, start to fly, and finally land again.

Discussion Introduce the idea of scary dragons and fearful dragons; what might a dragon be afraid of? Talk about how dragons exist in many, many cultures with many stories, masks and dances.

Activities Use the whiteboard for discussion of what dragons look like: their colours, scales, teeth. Using the card and colours:

- ✿ Invite everyone to create their own dragon mask, making sure there are large eye holes. Fasten the masks with elastic.
- ✿ Everyone wears their mask and walks around the room as their own individual dragon.
- ✿ In pairs, one is the dragon and other is something (or somebody) scared of the dragon; then swap roles.
- ✿ Still in pairs, one person is the dragon and the other is something (or somebody) that frightens the dragon; then swap roles.
- ✿ Make a dragon in pairs, using a large cloth and a mask. Move as a scary dragon, then as a frightened dragon; then swap roles.

> **Sharing** Everyone shares their masks in the big group and talks about how dragons have many different feelings.

> **Ending** Write or draw in journals or folders; relax with partner wrapped in fleeces.

Manage your Dragon

31

◯ Children ☑ Teenagers

Aims & Focus To support group members to strengthen their potential, but at the same time to understand both their limits and appropriate actions.

Materials Large whiteboard and markers, journals or folders, fleeces.

Warm-up Bring everyone into a seated circle for feedback and questions. Explain that the session will explore the great variety of dragon energy that people have. Think about the TV programme called 'The Dragon's Den' and its style of confrontation. Walk briskly around the room; on 'freeze', confront another person by the way you stand and gesture to them. Repeat several times and find different movements and stances.

Discussion Describe any confrontational behaviour, such as the sports teacher who snaps their fingers and points, rather than calling to someone by their name. How does it make people feel? Do they feel put-down or do they want to confront back? Write examples on the board.

Activities It is important to keep affirming strengths and successes.

✿ Remind the group that they can breathe in the positive and breathe out anything negative.

✿ Now breathe out positive dragon energy that warms and supports rather than destroys.

✿ Everyone imagines they are wearing their dragon T-shirt (see Part 3: Activity 21 'The Dragon T-shirt' and Worksheet 13) and walks around the room with confidence.

✿ In small groups create a role play called 'I can and I will', making sure that everyone has the opportunity to be positive.

✿ Show the role play to the group.

Sharing Build a whole group body sculpture (Resources: Body Sculpting) that shows the strengths and the progress of everyone.

Ending Write or draw in journals or folders, relax on, or under, fleeces.

Role Activities for Emotional Intelligence

Role-playing the Feelings Map

 Children Teenagers

Role Activities for Emotional Intelligence

> **Aims & Focus** Following on from the idea of drawing a map of feelings (Activity 22), the focus is on expanding awareness in a more social context and offering the group a chance to talk about how they feel about their own communities.

> **Materials** Large whiteboard and markers, hats and caps, shawls and material, journals or folders, fleeces.

Warm-up   Bring the group into a seated circle for feedback and questions. Introduce the idea that countries and communities can be mapped, as well as landscapes. Suggest that the group might create maps using body sculpting (see Resources: Notes on Body Sculpting). Create body sculpted maps that show areas in the community that might be 'cold', 'hot', 'tropical' or 'polar'.

Discussion   Invite the group to talk about the community where they live or where they used to live. What words would they use to describe the feelings and qualities in the community (e.g., downtrodden, angry, violent, hard-working, rich, stuck-up, snobby, happy, contented, bored, etc.); write the words on the whiteboard.

Activities   In pairs, encourage everyone to find ways to express the qualities that they have noticed in their communities.

- ✿ Experiment with body sculpting, without sound.
- ✿ Experiment with body sculpting, with sound.
- ✿ Use body sculpting to create a map of an area where different groups of people live. Think about the different qualities of these people.
- ✿ Encourage the partners to express their feelings to the rest of the group.
- ✿ Repeat, but ask them to explain why they feel this way about their communities.

> **Sharing** Coming back together as a group, explore how the small groups felt, and whether they learnt anything from each other.

> **Ending** Write or draw in journals or folders, and relax on, or under, fleeces.

Dramatising the Story 1

☑ Children ☑ Teenagers

Aims & Focus To bring together the several themes of feelings into a dramatised whole; to understand the flexibility of feelings and acknowledge the use of humour.

Materials Large whiteboard and marker, magazines with 'people' pictures showing expressive faces, journals or folders, fleeces.

Warm-up Bring everyone into a seated circle for feedback and questions. Introduce the idea of a story that shows different characters who express contrasting feelings. Run around the room and freeze when a character and feeling is called out, for example: 'bored teenager', 'scared grandmother', 'proud mother', 'shocked policeman or woman', and so on.

Discussion Explore the idea that when feelings are exaggerated we do not always take them seriously, and that people sometimes pretend to have certain feelings in order to get a reaction from others. Write any suggestions on the whiteboard.

Activities Invite everyone to work in small groups and experiment with the following ideas:

✪ One person directs the scene while another dramatises a feeling (e.g. sobs in an exaggerated way, but peeps through their fingers to see if it is having an effect); a third person takes it seriously.

✪ Repeat, but the third person does not take it seriously.

✪ Repeat, but the feeling is genuine and the third person still does not take it seriously.

✪ Repeat, but the feeling is genuine and the third person takes it seriously.

✪ Allow everyone to play different feelings and reactions.

Sharing Stay in small groups. Discuss real feelings and pretend feelings, and how they are experienced inside as well as to another person looking on. Bring ideas to the big group for further sharing.

Ending Write or draw in journals or folders; relax on, or under, fleeces.

Role Activities for Emotional Intelligence

34 Dramatising the Story 2

 Children Teenagers

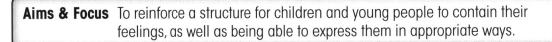

Aims & Focus To reinforce a structure for children and young people to contain their feelings, as well as being able to express them in appropriate ways.

Materials Large whiteboard and markers, Certificate of Achievement if it is the final session (see Worksheet 17), camera for recording presentation (if allowed), big drum, journals or folders.

Warm-up Bring everyone into a seated circle for feedback and questions. Acknowledge that this is the final session if it is the last one. Everyone scatters around the room and jumps away any surplus energy. Walking around the room, make a body sculpt of 'How I felt when I first came to the group'; more walking and another sculpt for 'How I felt when the group was difficult'; more walking and sculpting of 'How I feel at the end of the group' (See Resources: Body Sculpting).

Discussion Suggest that it is important to ask any questions or to clarify anything that has not been clear. Acknowledge the hard work and that work on feelings is not easy.

Activities Carry on from the warm-up idea that a range of feelings have been experienced by everyone. Suggest that pairs of group members might create a timeline that tells a story, in which one partner expresses the feelings non-verbally while the other partner gives the feelings words.

⚙ Work with a partner to talk about the range of feelings expressed during the course.

⚙ One person creates sculpts for their partner, to express a maximum of five of their own feelings (use the three situations explored in the warm-up).

⚙ Change around and repeat the activity.

⚙ Add words for the sculpts: 'When I first came here I was feeling ...', and so on. The partner creates the sculpts as they talk.

⚙ Change around and repeat the activity.

Sharing Share stories of 'My journey through the group' with the whole group and allow for comparing experiences. Acknowledge changes that people have experienced, and affirm the hard work.

Ending Presentation of Certificates if it is the final session. Final writing in journal and folders. Verbal acknowledgement of everyone in the room.

Role Activities for Emotional Intelligence

Part 5
Resources

Worksheets

Contract & Ground Rules for the Group

All Groups

Worksheet 1

Contract for the Group

We are attending the group on the following dates:

_____

We have not all chosen to be here,

Some of us are asked to be in this group.

We all agree to abide by the group rules as follows:

1 Everyone listens to what other people are saying without interrupting

2 Everyone agrees to behave in a respectful manner to others

3 Everyone agrees that there is no verbal or physical violence

4 Everyone agrees that equipment is not to be broken

5 _____

6 _____

7 _____

Signature or Thumb Print from all participants:

Contract & Ground Rules for the Group

All Groups

Agreement for Participating in the Group

I am participating in this group on the following dates:

_____

I agree to the following rules:

1   Showing respectful behaviour to others and listening to them.

2   Keeping control of any verbal or physical violence.

3   Cooperating with group members in the exercises.

4   A Personal rule for myself is … _____

5   _____

6   _____

Signed with name or picture:

Relationship Circles
(part 1)

Activities 3, 16, 18, 21, 28

Use the circle as a container for feelings or expressions, so that group members can learn to set boundaries. It can also be used to decorate group work (for instance, to make the badges in Activity 21 'Dragon T-shirt'), and could contain an important portrait (Activity 18 'Circles to Hug & Circles to Change', and Story Sheet 2: The Story of Olwen).

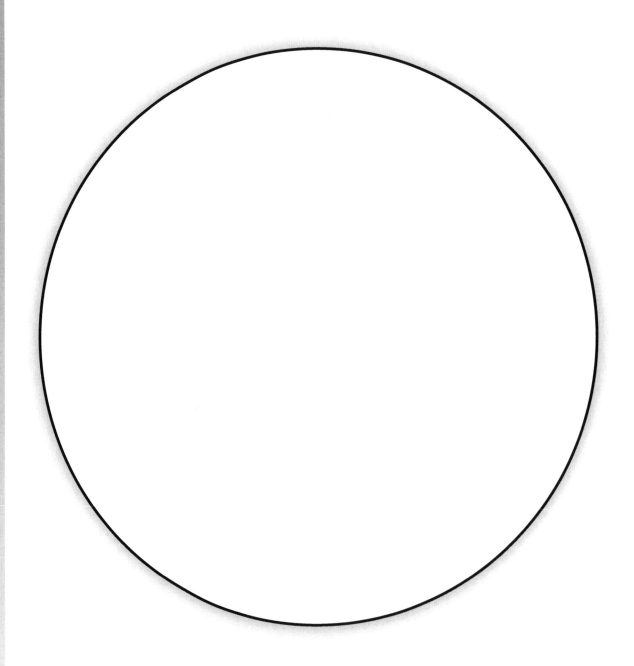

Worksheet 2

Relationship Circles
(part 2)

Activities 3, 16, 18, 21, 28

These circles are for exploration of 'people who are close to me' and 'people who are less close to me'. The inner and outer circles can also be used for exploring appropriate touch (Activities 18 'Circles to Hug & Circles to Change' and 28 'Hugging Who?').

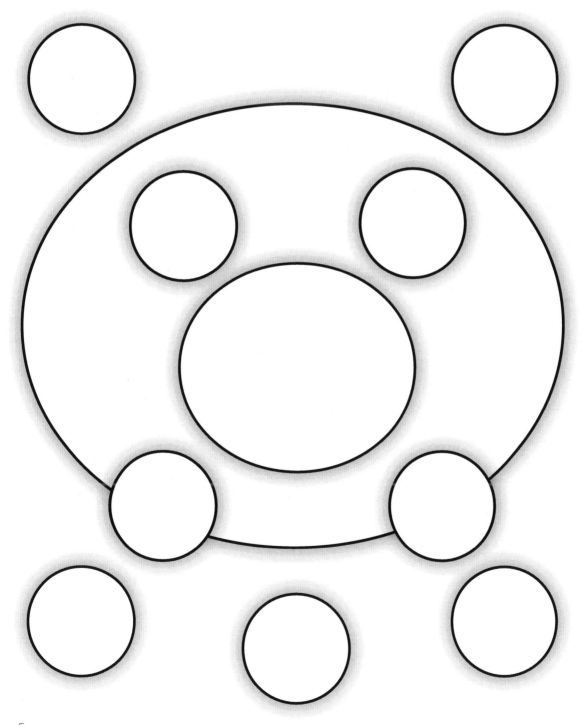

Recognising Primary Feelings: Anger

Activity 4

Read the statements below and think about whether they apply to you, then circle 'true' or 'untrue' for each one.

I have a lot of angry feelings.	true	untrue
When I express my anger I do it physically …	true	untrue
… against myself.	true	untrue
… against other people.	true	untrue
… by cutting myself or other actions.	true	untrue
When I express my anger, I do it vocally.	true	untrue
I scream and shout at others.	true	untrue
I scream, shout and cry on my own.	true	untrue

When you are feeling angry, what would be the most helpful thing that someone could say or do?

_____

Can you remember, when you look back, how long ago you started to feel angry?

_____

Was there something specific that made you angry?

_____

If yes, please draw a picture of your feelings about what happened.

It is important to tell a teacher or a friend how you are feeling: try not to bottle it up.

Worksheet 3

Recognising Primary Feelings: Sorrow or Sadness

> **Activity** 4

Read the statements below and think about whether they apply to you, then circle 'true' or 'untrue' for each one.

I have a lot of sad feelings.	true	untrue
When I express my sadness I do it physically …	true	untrue
… against myself.	true	untrue
… against other people.	true	untrue
… by cutting myself or other actions.	true	untrue
When I express my sadness I do it vocally.	true	untrue
I scream and cry at others.	true	untrue
I scream and cry on my own.	true	untrue

When you are feeling sad or sorrowful, what would be the most helpful thing that someone could say or do?

_____

Can you remember, when you look back, how long ago you started to feel sad?

_____

Was there a specific event that started off your feelings of sadness?

_____

If the answer is yes, please draw a picture that expresses how you are feeling.

It is important to tell a teacher or a friend how you are feeling: try not to bottle it up.

Worksheet 4

Recognising Primary Feelings: Surprise

Activity 4

Read the statements below and think about whether they apply to you, then circle 'true' or 'untrue' for each one.

I have a lot of surprised feelings.	true	untrue
When I express my surprise I do it physically ...	true	untrue
... against myself.	true	untrue
... towards other people.	true	untrue
When I express my surprise I do it vocally.	true	untrue
I call out to others.	true	untrue
I express my feelings to myself.	true	untrue

When you are feeling surprised, what would you like to happen next?

_____

Are there things that you would like to feel surprised about? Remember that surprises can be good or bad.

_____

_____

_____

It is important to tell a teacher or a friend how you are feeling: try not to bottle it up.

Worksheet 5

Recognising Primary Feelings: Joy or Happiness

Activity 4

Read the statements below and think about whether they apply to you, then circle 'true' or 'untrue" for each one.

I have a lot of happy feelings.	true	untrue
When I express my happiness I do it physically …	true	untrue
… towards myself.	true	untrue
… towards other people.	true	untrue
When I express my joy I do it vocally.	true	untrue
I scream and cry to others.	true	untrue
I scream and cry on my own.	true	untrue

When you are feeling joy or happiness, what would be the most helpful thing that you would like to do?

_____

Can you remember, when you look back, some early memories that were really happy ones?

_____

Can you recall one specific time that you were happy? Create a picture of it.

[ ]

It is important to tell a teacher or a friend how you are feeling: try not to bottle it up.

Worksheet 6

Recognising Primary Feelings: Fear & Being Scared

Worksheet 7

Activity 4

Read the statements below and think about whether they apply to you, then circle 'true' or 'untrue' for each one.

I have a lot of scared feelings.	true	untrue
When I express my fear I do it physically …	true	untrue
… against myself.	true	untrue
… towards other people.	true	untrue
… by cutting myself or other actions.	true	untrue
When I express my fear I do it vocally.	true	untrue
I shout and scream at others.	true	untrue
I express my feelings to myself.	true	untrue

When you are feeling frightened, what would you like other people to say or do?

_____

What is the first time that you can remember feeling scared?

_____

Draw a picture about being scared.

It is important to tell a teacher or a friend how you are feeling: try not to bottle it up.

Recognising Primary Feelings: Disgust

> **Activity** 4

Read the statements below and think about whether they apply to you, then circle 'true' or 'untrue" for each one.

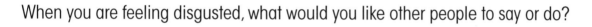

I have a lot of disgusted feelings.	true	untrue
When I express my disgust I do it physically …	true	untrue
… against myself.	true	untrue
… towards other people.	true	untrue
… by cutting myself or other actions.	true	untrue
When I express my disgust I do it vocally.	true	untrue
I shout and scream at others.	true	untrue
I express my feelings to myself.	true	untrue

When you are feeling disgusted, what would you like other people to say or do?

_____

What is the first time that you can remember feeling disgust?

_____

Draw a picture about being disgusted.

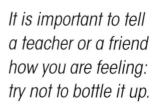

It is important to tell a teacher or a friend how you are feeling: try not to bottle it up.

Worksheet 8

 This page may be photocopied for instructional use only. *Creative Activities for Developing Emotional Intelligence* © Sue Jennings 2013

Foot Template (part 1)

Activities 15, 19, 25

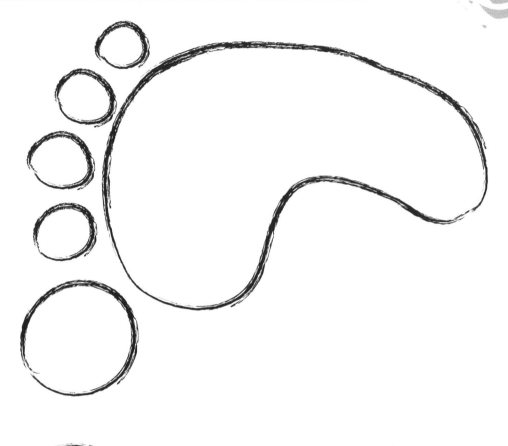

Foot Template (part 2)

The following expressions and exercises be used with Activities 15 'Preparation for Stability & Balance' and 25 'Stability & Balance', or developed in other ways. The expressions can also form the basis for discussion, or movement and drama work.

For example:

(i)   What does it mean if you 'put your foot down firmly'?

(ii) Walk round the room putting each foot down very firmly, then really stamp around the room, then walk very lightly. Think about how each movement feels, and then walk firmly around the space.

(iii) With a partner, think of someone who always puts their foot down firmly and discuss what sort of person they are.

(iv) Think of a story about this person and share it with the group or make a drama about the person's behaviour.

Some foot expressions:

Stand on your own two feet	One foot before the other
Put your foot down firmly	Feet of clay
Make a footprint	Feet don't touch the ground
Wrong-footed	Stand up for yourself
Two left feet	Stand up and be counted

Worksheet 9

Spiky & Jagged Feelings (part 1)

Activity 16

Sometimes our feelings can be 'spiky'. Look at the spiky wire below and decide whether it is to keep something in or to keep something out.

Draw a picture of your own spiky feelings; think about putting them inside a circle, then draw the circle.

Spiky & Jagged Feelings (part 2)

Activity 16

The jagged shapes can be used to express 'jagged' feelings through colouring and naming of the feelings.

My jagged feelings are _____

Activities 17, 29

These two pages on this worksheet can be used to focus on self-esteem and 'feeling like a star', as well as to explore stories that have star themes.

Stars (part 2)

Activities 17, 29

Colour the stars to show how it feels to be the centre of the stars; there are other people who are close by and are also stars.

Activity	19	Story Sheet	1

Colour the stars so that they shine through a very dark sky.

The Dragon T-shirt

Activities 21,31

A Feelings Map (part 1)

Activities 12, 22

Use the map to colour in your own feelings and then make a colour code for the map using the boxes below.

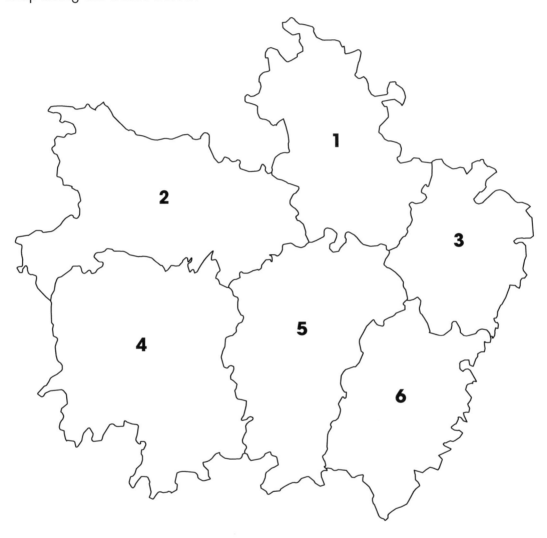

Colour in or number these boxes to show which colour represents which feeling.

Anger ☐   Happiness ☐

Fear ☐   Surprise ☐

Sadness ☐   Disgust ☐

A Feelings Map (part 2)

Activities 12, 22

This picture of a landscape can also be used for colouring in feelings. Where are the calm feelings or the scary ones or other sorts of feelings?

Activity 22

Use the heart to colour in your own feelings and then make a colour code for the heart using the boxes below.

Colour in these boxes to show which colour represents which feeling.

Anger ☐   Happiness ☐

Fear ☐   Surprise ☐

Sadness ☐   Disgust ☐

A Feelings Rainbow

Activity 22

Use the rainbow to colour in your own feelings and then make a colour code for the rainbow using the boxes below.

Colour in these boxes to show which colour represents which feeling.

Anger	☐	Happiness	☐
Fear	☐	Surprise	☐
Sadness	☐	Disgust	☐

Worksheet 16

Certificate of Achievement

Activity 34

Certificate

awarded to

_____

for attending the

Creative Activities Course

and showing changes in

1 _____

2 _____

3 _____

Signed _____

Project Leader

Date _____

Record & Assessment Sheet 1

Day-to-Day Embodiment

Embodied Responses	Responses in the Sessions		Responses at Home or in School	
1. Eye contact and gaze				
2. Eyes 'connected' with partner				
3. Appropriate touch				
4. Sexualised touch				
5. Whole body coordination				
6. Spatial awareness				
7. Balance				
8. Skipping and hopping				
9. Walking briskly and running				
10. Ticks or twitches				
11. Gesture with speech				
12. Repetitive/stereotyped movements				
Date: Participant's initials/code: Assessor's name:				

Worksheet 18

Record & Assessment Sheet 2

Creative Embodiment

Embodied Responses	Session One		Session Two	
1. Sensory play: hand cream, bubbles, sand, water				
2. Hand and finger games				
3. Trust games				
4. Capacity to focus				
5. Relaxation exercise				
6. Bodily tension				
7. Movement games (such as stop/start, Simon says)				
8. Movement with a partner/ moving against a partner				
9. Innovative movement and dance				
10. Copied movement and dance				
11. Mime and gesture				
12. Creative visualisation				

Date: Participant's initials/code: Assessor's name:

Worksheet 19

Record & Assessment Sheet 3

Creative Projection

Embodied Responses	Session One		Session Two	
1. Single large toy				
2. Single small toy				
3. Clay/plasticine/dough (shapes or named objects)				
4. Pencils/crayons				
5. Paint (finger and brush)				
6. Individual items or whole scene				
7. Balanced use of paper or small areas covered or over spilling				
8. Models and construction (card or bricks or kits)				
9. Puzzles				
10. Building houses/dens				
11. Puppets (finger/hand)				
12. Story telling with pictures or puppets				
Date: Participant's initials/code: Assessor's name:				

Ⓟ This page may be photocopied for instructional use only. *Creative Activities for Developing Emotional Intelligence* © Sue Jennings 2013

Record & Assessment Sheet 4

Creative Roles & Characters

Embodied Responses	Session One		Session Two	
1. Puppet with voice				
2. Puppet narrative				
3. Brief role play				
4. Development of a role				
5. Sustained role-play				
6. Use of masks				
7. Use of dressing up clothes and hats				
8. Use of props for a role				
9. Creation of a scene				
10. Creation of narrative with beginning, middle and end				
11. Transitions between everyday reality and dramatic reality				
12. Capacity to critically appraise dramatic work				
Date: Participant's initials/code: Assessor's name:				

Stories & Storytelling

We tell stories to an audience, and as storytellers we choose stories that we think that the listeners will enjoy hearing; there are times, too, when we wish to make a point of belief or fact. We may also choose stories as a means of clarifying or educating. Storytelling is something we do almost all the time in the way we communicate with others, as we become willing (or unwilling) listeners at the bus stop or surgery!

Stories have also been told for healing, as we know from the shaman and traditional midwives; indeed, parables and legends are famous for their use of metaphor in the healing or educational process. The storyteller adjusts the tale to suit the individual listener and this quality of fine-tuning is crucial in telling a good story.

Storytelling is important in emotional literacy as a story can give voice to feelings that an individual may not be able to express. It can also demonstrate appropriate emotional responses in different situations.

A story can be created in response to the particular needs of an individual or group. There may be feelings of extreme fear, being overwhelmed, hopelessness, futility or anger. People may be locked into destructive repetitive cycles or have very low self-esteem. Communities may be neglecting their traditional ethos and their care for each other, or turning a blind eye to unacceptable behaviour. The story may occur spontaneously, 'in the moment', or may be planned for a particular situation. Existing stories can also be used as templates for enhancing the emotional literacy of an individual or group.

Structuring your stories for children & teenagers

✿ Introduce the possibility of the wise person or animal, somebody 'street-wise' who has been there themselves (very popular with teenagers). It may be a very ordinary person, or another child or teenager (see Jennings 2010 for some helpful suggestions on building stories).

✿ Choose stories that take time to puzzle out.

✿ Make use of repetition, chants and rituals.

✿ Use a familiar structure, as in a fairy tale, but give it distance from the listener's own direct experience.

✿ Puppets, drama and ritual objects are all ways of exploring stories.

✿ Include the possibility of gradual change and understanding, rather than a sudden impact.

The ending of the story It is important to have a closure and resolution when the story finishes. It may introduce an interactive element (for example, 'So what do you think the child did next?'). The ending, however, needs to include changes from old beliefs to the new: 'So John was surprised when the old man smiled, he usually looked cross.' This type of story introduces a mindful way of thinking about the self, the family, the school, the world, and it is hoped that the new thinking will make an impact on destructive feelings or actions or behaviour. The story may need to be told more than once.

After the story The story can be dramatised as a play or even painted or danced. It can have a 'next instalment'. The story can be written out for the child or teenager for them to keep. It is important to remember that if you create a story for a particular individual it is in fact a gift to them, and care must be taken not just to repeat it elsewhere in its original form.

Remember that children and teenagers may wish to illustrate their stories, as this helps to make them their own. The following stories have been specifically chosen for the development of Emotional Intelligence. The story itself will make an impact and this will be enhanced if the story is explored through movement, art or drama.

The Story of Star Woman (page 1)

Many years ago there was a race of people whose home was in the stars and they were self-sufficient, apart from having no milk. They were a very peaceful people and lived in harmony with each other. Every Star Woman had a special basket that she was given in her teens.

Regularly the Star Women would come down to earth on silver threads from the stars, with buckets to milk the cows on the farmsteads, and then take the milk back to the stars.

There was a farmer who lived alone with his farm and cattle; he was so lonely without someone to share his life. He was worried that his milk kept disappearing, and so one night he decided to stay up and watch over his cattle. He hid in a bush at the edge of the field. The night was very dark and he was uncomfortable. He was about to give up and go home when he heard a sound in the distance: it was a tinkly sound of laughter.

It came closer and, peering through the bush, he saw silver threads coming down to earth and a group of women chattering and laughing together. They were carrying their buckets and walking to the field, to his cows. He went towards the women, desperate for their company. He wanted to talk to them, but when they saw him they ran back to their silver threads and went back to the stars.

All except one who stumbled; by the time she had found her balance again, her thread had disappeared without her. The farmer went up to her and asked her to stay and live on his farm. She agreed, but on one condition: he must never ask to look inside the basket. He promised to respect her wishes and they started to create a life together.

The basket stood in the corner of the living room. Star Woman settled into the farming life and she had her own garden where she grew plants and flowers. Sometimes at twilight she would stand a little wistfully at the door of the house and gaze up at the stars, wondering whether her friends and family could see her and whether they missed her.

Story Sheet 1

1 The Story of Star Woman (page 2)

The farmer was very happy, but he began to feel curious about Star Woman's basket, he kept wondering what was inside and in the end he could bear it no longer. He stole back into the house, wrenched off the lid and looked inside – and then burst out laughing! He turned and Star Woman was standing in the doorway.

'But you promised,' she said, 'You gave me your word.'

'But there is nothing in the basket,' said the farmer, and he laughed again.

Star Woman did not say anything more. She turned on her heel and went out through the front door; when she reached the gate she stopped. A silver thread was hanging there in front of her …

Reflections

Allow some group time for talking about the story before addressing the questions and activities below. How might Star Woman been feeling so far away from her home? Maybe her family could see her when the stars came out at night? How did Star Woman feel that he had broken his promise? Why was the farmer feeling so lonely? Why could he not see what was in the basket?

1 What is the Star Woman feeling when she sees the farmer open her basket?

2 What is the farmer feeling when she walks away?

3 Does the Star Woman return to the stars?

4 Colour the Worksheet 15 'Carpet of Stars'.

5 Create an ending to the story and draw a picture.

6 Draw Star Woman's basket with a tight lid, and handles, so she can carry it on her back.

7 Decide what she carries in the basket that is so precious.

8 Create a drama about the ending of the story.

The Story of Olwen
(page 1)

Olwen was an ancient sun goddess who was celebrated as the Queen of the May. Wherever she walked, white flowers would spring up in her path, so she was also known as 'Olwen of the white footprints'.

There are many stories about Olwen, but this is her love story: it is the story of how Olwen fell in love with Cullwch and of Cullwch, her beloved, who had to succeed at many tasks before he could marry her.

Culhwch was the cousin of King Arthur, about whom you know many, many tales. Culhwch fell in love with Olwen at first sight, because her beauty was so dazzling. She wore red silks and gold jewellery that was studded with precious stones. Her hair was yellow and her cheeks were rosy, and many men before Culhwch had fallen in love with her. However, Olwen loved only Culhwch.

Olwen's father was the giant Ysbaddeden, whose name means 'Giant Hawthorn Tree', and he forbade the marriage. Ysbaddeden was huge – one of the largest giants in history – and feared by many, especially as he could roar so loudly that the rocks would crack. His eyelids were so heavy that two of his servants held them up with pitchforks.

Olwen kept trying to persuade her father to allow her to marry Culhwch. In the end he agreed, providing that Culhwch completed some difficult tasks. When he mentioned these tasks, Ysbaddeden raised his eyebrows so high that everyone shook with fear. Olwen just gave her father a wink, and he was so surprised that he actually smiled!

There were thirteen difficult and dangerous tasks that Culhwch had to complete before the marriage could take place. They included stealing the enormous sword from the Giant Wrach, finding Mabon, who had disappeared as a child and was being kept in a watery prison, and bringing back the tusk of the mighty wild boar known as Ysgithyyrwyn. However, Ysbaddeden had not realised that Culhwch had strong and powerful relatives who were prepared to help him. King Arthur and his followers assisted Culhwch to complete all the tasks. Olwen's father was very surprised.

Olwen became the wife of Culhwch for ever, and continued to leave a trail of flowery white footprints whenever she walked on the grass.

2 The Story of Olwen
(page 2)

Reflections

Allow some group time for talking about the story before addressing the questions and activities below. How might Olwen feel about her father being so strict? But she got him to smile, would that be unusual? What other ways might she persuade her father to be less angry? How would the giant feel after Culhwch had completed the tasks? Would Culhwch want to change his mind once the giant had given him the conditions?

1 Walk around the room as an enormous giant with heavy limbs that can scarcely move; give a very loud roar that could crack rocks.

2 Pick up an large imaginary rock, and slowly heave it down the mountain.

3 Sit with a partner; think about the tasks that Culhwch had to complete; create some more tasks and share them with the group.

4 Imagine you are a giant who is so large you cannot move your own body – draw your portrait as a giant.

5 Create a group picture of Olwen's white footprints across a field. Think about white flowers that grow among grass, such a clover.

6 In threes, role-play a scene where Culhwch has to persuade Arthur to help him with the dangerous tasks, and the third person also tries to persuade him

7 Vary the scene so that one person tried to stop Arthur from agreeing as it is going to be too dangerous.

8 Create a silly scene where Culhwch asks Arthur's help for ridiculous tasks such as eating a bowl of corn-flakes blindfolded, and Arthur has to say no because they are difficult tasks. The rule is that nobody must laugh!

The Story of the Rainbow Silk (page 1)
(adapted from an ancient Persian tale)

In ancient times there was a young prince who spent most of his time being very bored with life. He seemed to have everything that he wanted and he was still not satisfied. The members of his staff were at their wits end to know what was the best thing to do.

His faithful advisor with a long grey beard kept trying to find new and interesting things for the prince to experience, but to no avail. One day the prince said that the advisor had to find something new to interest him – or there would be trouble!

The advisor went to the kitchens and spoke to the cooks and said that they had to produce something very special by the following morning and after some protest they agreed.

He then went to talk to the carpenters and said that they must produce something new and different by the next morning – or there would be trouble! They were shocked at the length of time that they had been given to come up with something special, but the advisor persuaded them to be ready at the palace gates the next morning.

Finally he went to see the musicians and asked them to compose new music for the prince, and they said it was impossible in such a short space of time. The advisor said that their very lives could depend on it and that they must try. So the musicians said that they would stay up all night and do their best.

Wearily the advisor went home to bed and dozed very fitfully until dawn. When the sun came up, he looked out of his window in the turret and there were the cooks and the carpenters and the musicians all lined up outside the palace gates. They went in through the great studded doors into the prince's presence where he was lounging on a couch.

The Story of the Rainbow Silk (page 2)

The cooks presented their food and the prince shouted at them and said it was boring; the carpenters carried in the most beautiful carved box you have ever seen, inlaid with mother-of-pearl, and he chased them out of the room. The musicians sang their new song for the prince and he shouted at them to disappear because the sound they made was so dreadful.

Everyone slunk home in disappointment and the prince called the advisor. He said that the advisor had to find something new or there would be very great trouble and he was giving him one last chance. The advisor was very fearful because the prince was SO angry – he even feared he might lose his head.

This time the advisor went to see the clowns and the poets and the astronomers and pleaded with them all to create something new for the prince by the following morning. He emphasised that they would all be in great trouble otherwise. And the next morning they were all there with special gifts for the prince. Again the prince became angry and said that the clowns were not funny, while the poets were not poetic. The astronomers had found a new star and named it after him – but the prince astonished the room by shouting that he did not want to be a small star amongst millions!

The advisor became very fearful and pleaded to the prince for one last chance. He went to his turret and sat in his chair looking out over the city. He felt at his wits end, and the tears streamed down his face and trickled through his long grey beard.

Then, as he looked through his tears, he began to form an idea that perhaps could work. He wiped his eyes and went out into the dark night, making for the workshop of the silk weavers. He explained his idea and they were very intrigued. But when the advisor said that it had to be completed by the very next morning they were aghast. The weavers said that it was quite impossible, but the advisor silenced them and said that everyone's lives depended on it.

The Story of the Rainbow Silk (page 3)

He went home with a heavy heart and did not sleep very much. In the morning he looked out of his window and saw that the silk weavers were indeed there at the gates. He went down and joined them as they were ushered into the presence of the prince. The prince looked more bored than ever as they entered, bearing a large roll of material between them.

They unfurled the silk on floor in front of the prince and explained that it was rainbow silk, woven especially for the prince. There was complete silence as everyone waited for his response – and the advisor became extremely nervous.

The prince got up slowly and picked up the end of the silk; he wrapped it around his shoulders and walked around the room. Then he did a little dance, swirling the silk as he went, and it shimmered and shone in the beams of light coming through the windows.

He came to a halt, looked slowly around the room full of anxious faces, and told them that he realised he had treated them all most cruelly by rejecting all the good things they had done for him. He was truly sorry for behaving so badly and would try to make amends. By way of showing how sorry he was, he decreed that everyone in the city could now wear rainbow silk, which they did, most joyously.

Suddenly the advisor remembered that the night before he had seen rainbow colours through his tears when he had been so distressed in his room. And he realised it had been the rainbow colours of his tears that had inspired the weavers to make rainbow silk.

And that was how the prince and all the people of his city became joyous, now that they were wearing their rainbow-coloured silk.

Story Sheet 3

3 The Story of the Rainbow Silk (page 4)

Reflections

Allow some group time for talking about the story before addressing the questions and activities below. What might have caused this young man to become so bored? Had he inherited this kingdom when his father died? Did he have brothers and sisters and, if so, where are they? An old man and a young man are in charge of running the kingdom; might there be others who are part of a council or government?

1 What had happened to the prince's parents?

2 Did the old man really feel scared that he would die?

3 Was everyone in the city and the palace used to being asked to do these tasks, or was this the first time?

4 Draw a picture of an eastern city with a skyline of turrets.

5 Draw a beautiful tile that could have been on the walls or floor of the palace.

6 Think about the fact that the old man's tears inspired him to find a solution to the difficulties; can tears be an inspiration?

7 Create a play where people bring gifts and the prince rejects them.

8 Dramatise a meeting between the different crafts people to complain about the pressure to do everything in a hurry and during the night. What will they do about it?

Story Sheet 3

The Child Who Disappeared (page 1)

The forest family was sitting around a table, peeling mushrooms they had picked that day. Outside there a storm was raging, and the wind was howling against the windows. The rain poured down in sheets as if the sky had burst.

There was a tap at the window and the door opened; their cousin came in, dripping wet, in a large yellow raincoat.

'I've bought you a visitor,' she said.

'Who is that?' asked Mamma.

'You can't see her,' said the cousin. 'She has lived so long with her ironical, cold aunt, that she is invisible; her aunt put a bell around her neck so that she knows where she is.'

Sure enough, they all heard a tinkly sound crossing the room to the fire, and saw wet foot prints on the floor.

'I must be going,' said the cousin, and she went out into the dark night again.

Mamma decided to prepare a room for the child and placed an apple and a warm drink by the bedside. She lit a candle and noticed a little bump appear under the bed cover and a small dent on the pillow.

Not a word was said, and Mamma went downstairs and sat long into the night, reading Grandmother's recipe book. She searched for a recipe to make someone visible again: 'If people get misty and difficult to see …' she read. 'Right,' she said, and started to mix the medicine for the new family member.

The next morning down the stairs came two little brown feet and the sound of the tinkling bell; Mamma, Poppa and the children noticed. The child ate some breakfast, and then the whole family went out to the orchard. It was apple-picking day, and

The Child Who Disappeared (page 2)

there was apple-cheese to be made. They lit a fire and, as the children picked the apples, Mamma minced them and cooked them in her big pot. The child was so excited that she knocked the pot over; immediately she became completely invisible again.

Mamma said, 'If you want the earth to grow something for you, then you have to give it a present; that is what my Grandma used to say.' Immediately the feet and then the legs of the child became visible. Everyone continued the picking and the cooking until bedtime.

That night Mamma took off her red petticoat and made it into a little dress and a hairband for the child, and left them by the side of her bed. The next morning the child came down the stairs, wearing her new dress – and she was visible up to her neck.

The children decided that she could learn to play games with them and have some fun. It was very hard going as she had never played games before, and in the end one of the children shouted, 'You don't know how to play; no wonder you haven't got a face!'

Poppa decided it was time to go on a picnic to the seaside. They all piled into the noisy, bumpy old car, and when they got there the children played games on the sand. The child stayed near Mamma as she sat on the landing stage, dangling her legs in the water. The child turned around and noticed with horror that Poppa was creeping up behind Mamma and was about to push her into the water.

The child gave a snarl and bit Poppa, who toppled over and fell into the water. At that moment the very angry face of the child could be seen by everyone.

'Poppa was just pretending to push me in the water,' said Mamma, as Poppa tried to retrieve his wet hat. The child then laughed when she realised that Poppa had only been playing a game.

The Child Who Disappeared (page 3)

Reflections

Allow some group time for talking about the story before addressing the questions and activities below. How must the child have felt when she was invisible? Did her aunt have any regrets at being so sarcastic? Could the cousin have taken her anywhere else? What must it be like for this family to live in the forest, right away from other people?

1 Draw or paint a picture of a house in a forest.

2 Draw or paint one single mushroom in detail.

3 Create a picture of all the mushrooms on the table.

4 Why do you think the child became invisible?

5 Why was she being brought up by her aunt?

6 Role-play the scene where she becomes visible again.

7 Create a play with the scene from the orchard.

8 If there is a sand tray, play with the sand and think about the picnic on the beach; create the scene with small objects.

Story Sheet 4

5 The Butterfly Man
(page 1)

Long ago and far away, there lived two very beautiful sisters. Their beauty was famous all over the land and beyond. Many people came to visit them just to gaze, and there were others who wished to marry them.

The sisters were unaware of all the attention and they just felt that people were making a fuss. They were very busy with their task of trying to make life more beautiful for other people. They visited sick people and took them sweet-smelling flowers, and they spent time with old people (including their grandmothers), and fed them delicate food that tasted so special. And they went to see poor families and took them clothes – not 'hand-me-downs', which is what the poor people were always given – but something new and very special, and made of fine cloth.

A young man in the next village was a constant visitor; his heart went out to the sisters and he loved them both. One day he loved one and the next day he loved the other; would he ever have the chance to choose between them?

The sisters took no notice of him at all, and he was deeply troubled. Surely one of them would just look up and give him a smile? But no, there was not even a greeting; it was as if the sisters did not see him.

For many days he thought about what he could do, and in the end he changed himself into a very beautiful butterfly with amazing colours. He then flew past the sisters and immediately they looked up and said to each other, 'What a beautiful butterfly – it must be the most beautiful I have ever seen!' And they nodded together and agreed.

The young man was well pleased and went home and slept soundly. The next day he went back to the sisters, hoping that now he could get to know them better. To his horror they were in deep conversation with a large white butterfly and took no notice of him at all. He was very, very angry and decided that he would kill the white butterfly – then surely he would be seen again.

He killed the white butterfly, and the most enormous cloud of beautiful butterflies was released all over the land.

The Butterfly Man
(page 2)

Reflections

Allow some group time for talking about the story before addressing the questions and activities below. It often takes a while for the quirky ending to this story to make an impact. It is adapted from a story told by Native Americans to young people as they set out on their life's path. Think about all the kind things that the sisters did, almost too good to be true! How is the young man feeling in his heart when he realises that he wants to kill the white butterfly?

1 Draw or paint as many butterflies as will fill up a page.

2 Think about the rest of the family. Were the two sisters orphans? Who had brought them up?

3 Think about any time in your life when you have wanted something or someone so desperately – in what part of your body did you feel it? Did you do anything about it? Did you tell anybody?

4 For young children, create the story using movement and symbolic gestures, with light cloths for the butterfly wings.

5 Create a group collage of the things and people you feel are beautiful.

6 Create a play about the story, being careful to use symbolic gestures, especially for the killing.

7 Discuss what might have happened next in this story? How did it finally end?

Drama & Focus Games

These games can be used in their own right or incorporated into your session plans based on the first four sections of the book. Many of the games can be used as warm-up activities or to help groups to concentrate. They are also useful when groups are 'all over the place', as they bring together both physical and mindful action, and rely on mutual endeavour for them to succeed. It is also important to encourage participants to bring their own games from the playground or drama class and to have the confidence to show them to others, coaching them until the games are carried out accurately.

These activities can help:

1 to promote concentration and attention;

2 to develop cooperation and collaboration;

3 to place limits on behaviour;

4 to contain excess emotions;

5 to utilise energy; and

6 to build confidence and self-esteem.

The ideas for these games have grown from many people's creativity as well as my own: Augusto Boal, Veronica Sherborne, Ros Johnson, Andy Hickson, Frantic Assembly, as well as participants themselves.

1 Push Me – Pull You

Work in pairs with a partner of similar height. Place both hands on each other's shoulders and try to push each other across the room. Encourage partners to keep feet firmly on the floor, knees slightly bent. Repeat by holding hands and pulling partners, again trying to keep feet firmly on the floor.

2 One-at-a-Time

The whole group stands in a large circle and, one by one, takes a step forward. If two people step forward at the same time, the game has to start again. The game is complete when everyone has stepped forward one person at a time. The game can be repeated in reverse with everyone stepping back, one person at a time.

3 Advanced One-at-a-Time

Start by standing in a large circle; sit down one by one. If two people sit down at the same time, the game starts again. Repeat in reverse and stand up, one person at a time.

4 Heigh-Ho!

Everyone sits in a circle and each person has a wooden spoon. Hold up the spoon in your right hand and bring it down when you sing 'Heigh-Ho'. Then pass the spoon to the right and receive the spoon from the left, in rhythm, while singing, 'Heigh-Ho, Heigh-Ho, it's off to work we go, to keep on singing all the day'. Then pass spoon right and left between your own hands on 'Heigh-Ho, Heigh-Ho, Heigh-Ho'. Repeat the actions, passing the spoon to the right (and receiving from the left), with the words, 'Heigh-Ho, Heigh-Ho, it's off to work we go, with a knife and fork and belly of pork'. Then then pass between your own hands again, singing 'Heigh-Ho, Heigh-Ho, Heigh-Ho'. Usually there is a lot of laughter and one person ends up with all the spoons; but, once perfected, the game gives focus and rhythm.

5 Lines

Everyone stands in a line, with the oldest at one end and the youngest at the other, noting who is on either side of them. (This is Line One.) Stand in a line with the tallest at one end and shortest at the other, noting how people either side have changed (this is Line Two). Stand in a line with birthdays in January at one end and December at the other, again noting the changes (Line Three). From time to time call out 'Line One' (or Two or Three) and everyone has to form that line again.

6 Clear the Space

Call out 'clear the space', and everyone runs to the sides of the room and presses against a wall (not a window). Call out 'find the centre' and everyone has to huddle in the middle of the room taking up as little space as possible. Call out 'heads on shoulders' and everyone places their head on the shoulder of the person nearest to them. It is important that these things are done as three separate actions.

7 Keep the Knot

Everyone stands in a large circle holding hands. Gradually create a group knot by going over, under, and through each other, until there is no more space, but hands are still held. Then unravel the knot without breaking the hands. Often it will end with everyone or one person facing outwards, and the skill lies in working out how to bring it back to everyone facing inwards.

8 Dead Lions

Everyone lies on the floor as if they are dead lions, and if their breathing can be seen they are out. A simple exercise for calming and resting!

9 Remember the Steps

Everyone has one minute to: run to all corners of the room, jump three times, and touch five pairs of knees. Stop. Then everyone has to retrace their steps and actions.

10 Newspaper Islands

Place pieces of newspaper around the room, and everyone has to run around the 'islands' until there is a drumbeat, when they stand still on a piece of newspaper. Gradually decrease the size or numbers of the pieces; everyone has to assist each other to stay on the increasingly tiny bits of paper or balance together on the reducing numbers of islands.

11 Bodies on Floor

In group of three, create a sculpture with only three feet touching the floor. Then create a sculpture with two feet and two hands touching the floor. Experiment with other combinations.

12 Grandmother's Footsteps

Always popular with younger children and enhances concentration and observation. One person is grandmother and the remainder slowly creep up behind her and try to reach her without being seen. Grandmother turns around from time to time, and any one she sees moving has to go back to the beginning. (Play Grandfather's Footsteps with boys.)

13 I Saw an Elephant on the Way to School

One person is the teacher and one person is the pupil who is late for school. The pupil goes out of the room, while the group decide on a ridiculous reason for their lateness. The group stand behind the teacher's chair and mimes to the pupil why they are late. From time to time the teacher looks around, and anyone caught moving is out. The game is finished when the pupil knows the reason for their lateness, which can be as fantastic as the group decide.

14 Follow My Hand

Working in pairs, one person holds their hand out and walks backwards around the room while the other person follows them, keeping their eye on the hand. Change around.

15 The Mirror

Working in pairs, one person is the mirror and copies the actions of the person looking in the mirror. The aim is to synchronise the movements as closely as possible. Change around.

16 Animal Chaos!

Everyone in the group stands in the circle, chooses an animal and decides what sound it makes. Encourage variety, from tiger to ant. Have a few practice runs. Then add a movement as well as sound. If 'jungle' is called out, everyone expresses sound and movement; if 'all change' is called out, everyone changes animal with a person on their right; if a single animal's name is called out, then that animal must make its sound and movement and everyone has to copy.

17 Radio Channels

Brainstorm different radio channels, their names and what they broadcast: speaking clock, chat shows, music (of different kinds), stories, news, or even a police channel. Everyone chooses a channel and practises a few phrases or sounds appropriate to that channel. One person stands in the middle of the circle and slowly points to first one channel, and then another. Each 'channel' continues broadcasting until the person in the middle of the circle switches it off by turning away.

18 Human Postcards

In small groups, create a picture postcard as a body sculpt. Other group members have to guess where the place is.

19 Postcard Role Play

Pre-prepare some typical phrases written on backs of postcards: 'Wish you were here'; 'This place is amazing, the food is out of this world'; 'Terrible hotel, the drains are all blocked'; and 'I can see orange trees out of my window'. Each small group has a phrase and creates a scene that might happen on the holiday, then shares their scene with the others.

20 Holiday Story

One person tells the story of their holiday and uses members of the group to body sculpt the words, for example:

> 'I went on holiday to Brighton and it rained [sculpt person as the rain, just whispering the word 'rain' to them]; there was a huge dinosaur [sculpt someone as a dinosaur] in the park ...'

At the end the group should be able to tell the story of the person's holiday.

Notes on Body Sculpting

This technique is extremely useful because it enables children and young people to communicate an idea, a feeling or a shape through their bodies. A sculpt can be made by one person, or any number up to five, (beyond that it can become chaotic unless a group is used to working in this way). Invite members of the group to create for example, an angry body-shape in pairs. This is sculpting through the body. Many of the worksheets incorporate body-sculpting ideas to help stimulate emotional awareness, and the way emotions are communicated through the body.

Notes on Sand Play

In order to create situations and stories through sand play, it is important to work with small numbers of participants. I would suggest six to eight as a maximum. Place sand trays on small tables in a circle so that people are looking inwards. I use the circular trays from garden centres for holding large plant pots, so that each sand tray is approximately 18" in diameter. Play sand is very fine and has been sterilised, and there should be at least 2 inches in the tray. Have a collection of toys and miniatures, including diverse, ethnically mixed people, male and female, people with disabilities (story characters, mythic figures, ordinary occupations, young old, with children and babies); assorted animals, including wild and fierce creatures as well as pets and farm animals; fences, trees, shells, coins, large buttons. Over time I have collected other objects such as souvenir small pots, little bells, religious figures (representing all belief systems).

Start the session by reminding the group that it is time for them to be reflective about themselves and to use the sand play as a way of showing a story. Before the activity starts, encourage everyone to deep-breath several times and to focus their attention on working quietly with the materials available.

Each person is invited to choose up to ten objects with which to create their story. It is important to emphasise that the stories are spontaneous and can be on any theme. Sometimes they are highly personal and show a current event or conflict, at other times they are symbolic and obviously have meaning to the individual. It is also important to repeat that the group is confidential and material from other people's stories is not to be repeated outside the room.

Allow for roughly 20 minutes for the creation of the story and then 20 minutes for sharing the stories in the group. No-one is obliged to tell their story, they can just show the picture they have created. Ten minutes is needed to dismantle and de-role the figures and replace them where they came from. Invite sharing if anyone wants to say anything, and end with a deep breathing exercise.

Breathing Exercises

Breathing is at the heart of creative activity and tension reduction. Taking a deep breath can stop people reacting in the heat of the moment, and often inappropriately. It is also healthy to encourage deep breathing exercises as it both calms the feelings as well as increasing the oxygen in the blood-stream. It is interesting to note that breathing features strongly in ante-natal classes and child-birth. People have to be taught *how* to breathe deeply, to shallow breathe and to breathe for effort. Very small children get into breathing patterns, often stemming from their birth experience (maybe they were made to breathe by the mid-wife or doctor) and early holding can establish even breathing patterns. Books on voice have many exercises for breathing (Berry 2000) and demonstrate simple breathing routines that are accessible for everyone.

For example: Breathe in through the nose and blow slowly out through the mouth, 3 times. Repeat the exercise and after breathing in, hold the breath for a count of three, before breathing out again.

Take a very deep breath and then say the word home as strongly as possible (this expels stale air from the lungs), repeat twice.

Further Reading

Berry C., 2000, *Your Voice & How to Use It*, Random House, London.

Bowlby J., 1965, *Child Care and the Growth of Love*, Penguin, London.

Bowlby J., 2005, *The Making and Breaking of Affectional Bonds*, Routledge, London (first published 1979, Tavistock, London).

Bradberry T., Greaves J. & Lencioni P.M., 2009, *Emotional Intelligence 2.0*, TalentSmart, San Diego.

Cozolino L., 2002, *The Neuroscience of Psychotherapy*, Norton, London.

Damasio A., 2000, *The Feeling of What Happens*, Vintage, London.

Erikson E., 1995, *Childhood and Society*, Vintage, London (first published 1950, Norton, New York).

Gerhardt S., 2004, *Why Love Matters: How Affection Shapes a Baby's Brain*, Brunner-Routledge, Hove.

Goleman D., 2004, *Emotional Intelligence, and Working with Emotional Intelligence*, Bloomsbury, London & New York.

Goleman D., 2006, *Social Intelligence: the New Science of Human Relationships*, Hutchinson, London.

Gunaratana B.H., 2002, *Mindfulness in Plain English*, Wisdom Publications, Boston.

Hickson A., 2011, *How to Stop Bullying: 101 Strategies that really work*, Speechmark, Milton Keynes.

Hughes D., 2006, *Building the Bond of Attachment: Awakening Love in Deeply Troubled Children*, Jason Aronson, Lanham, MD.

Jennings S., 1990, *Dramatherapy with Families, Groups and Individuals*, Jessica Kingsley, London.

Jennings S., 1998, *Introduction to Dramatherapy: Ariadne's Ball of Thread*, Jessica Kingsley, London.

Jennings S., 1999, *Introduction to Developmental Play Therapy: Playing and Health*, Jessica Kingsley, London.

Jennings S., 2005, *Creative Play with Children at Risk*, Speechmark, Milton Keynes.

Jennings S., 2008, 'Project WOW! Creative Programme for Excluded Children'. Rowan, Glastonbury.

Jennings, S. 2010 *StoryBuilding: 100+ Ideas for Building Story and Narrative Skills*, Hinton House, Buckingham.

Jennings S., 2011a, *Healthy Attachments and Neuro-Dramatic-Play*, Jessica Kingsley, London.

Jennings S., 2011b, *The Anger Management Toolkit: Understanding and Transforming Anger in Children and Adolescents*, Hinton House, Buckingham.

Jennings S., 2011c, *101 Activities for Empathy and Awareness*, Hinton House, Buckingham.

Jennings S., 2012a, *Neuro-Dramatic-Play Part One*, The Healing Tree, Somerset.

Jennings S., 2012b, *Neuro-Dramatic-Play and Trauma*, B. Braun & The Healing Tree, Malaysia & Somerset.

Jennings S., 2012c, 'Drama Therapy Assessment Through Embodiment-Projection-Role (EPR), in *Assessment in Drama Therapy*, eds, Johnson D.L., Pendzik S. & Snow S. Charles C. Thomas, Springfield.

Jennings S., 2013, *101 Activities for Managing Challenging Behaviour*, Hinton House, Buckingham.

Mead G.H., 1934, *Mind, Self and Society*, University of Chicago Press, Chicago.

Pendzik S., 2008, 'Using the 6-key Model as an intervention tool in drama therapy', in *The Arts in Psychotherapy*, 35, 349–354.

Sherborne V., 2001, *Developmental Movement for Children*, Worth Reading, London.

Siegal D.J., 2007, *The Mindful Brain: Reflection and Attunement in the Cultivation of Well – Being*, W.W. Norton, London/New York.

Smith S.D., 2012, *Sandtray Play and Storymaking*, Jessica Kingsley, London.

Stein S.J., 2009, *Emotional Intelligence for Dummies*, John Wiley, Ontario, Canada.

Steiner C., 2003, *Emotional Literacy: Intelligence with a Heart*, Personhood Press, Fawnskin, Ca.

Sunderland M., 2006, *What Every Parent Needs to Know*, Dorling-Kindersley, London.

Williams M., 2007, *The Mindful Way through Depression*, Guilford Press, New York.

Useful websites

www.suejennings.com

www.actionwork.com

www.dramatherapy.net

www.antiviolencecampus.org

101 Activities & Ideas

* Creative and practical solutions to issues around emotional well-being in young people. Many teachers, care workers and therapists are challenged by difficult behaviours, and families often feel lost for solutions to sudden outbursts or young people's feelings of alienation and lack of self-esteem.

* Containing a host of ideas for home, school and youth groups, the books will help to tackle these difficult issues in a positive and active way. There are no magic answers, but the ideas aim to empower young people to find solutions to some of their own difficulties, while providing guidance for more positive directions.

* The books adopt a 'hands-on' approach with a firm and enabling attitude and provide a sound practical basis for active intervention for behaviour change.

**101 Activities for
Empathy & Awareness**
ISBN: 978-1-906531-33-1

**101 Activities for Social
& Emotional Resilience**
ISBN: 978-1-906531-46-1

**101 Ideas for Managing
Challenging Behaviour**
ISBN: 978-1-906531-44-7

**101 Activities for Increasing
Focus & Motivation**
ISBN: 978-1-906531-45-4

**101 Activities for Positive
Thoughts & Feelings**
ISBN: 978-1-906531-47-8

www.hintonpublishers.com